ESCAPE
the Coming
NIGHT

A Message of Hope
in a Time of Crisis

Study Guide–Volume 2

DAVID JEREMIAH

with Dr. David Jeremiah

Contents

ABOUT
DR. DAVID JEREMIAH
AND TURNING POINT

D r. David Jeremiah is the founder of Turning Point, a ministry committed to providing Christians with sound Bible teaching relevant to today's changing times through radio and television broadcasts, audio series, books, and live events. Dr. Jeremiah's common-sense teaching on topics such as family, prayer, worship, angels, and biblical prophecy forms the foundation of Turning Point.

David and his wife, Donna, reside in El Cajon, California, where he serves as the senior pastor of Shadow Mountain Community Church. David and Donna have four children and twelve grandchildren.

In 1982, Dr. Jeremiah brought the same solid teaching to San Diego television that he shares weekly with his congregation. Shortly thereafter, Turning Point expanded its ministry to radio. Dr. Jeremiah's inspiring messages can now be heard worldwide on radio, television, and the Internet.

Because Dr. Jeremiah desires to know his listening audience, he travels nationwide holding ministry events that touch the hearts and lives of many people. According to Dr. Jeremiah, "At some point in time, everyone reaches a turning point; and for every person, that moment is unique, an experience to hold onto forever. There's so much changing in today's world that sometimes it's difficult to choose the right path. Turning Point offers people an understanding of God's Word as well as the opportunity to make a difference in their lives."

Dr. Jeremiah has authored numerous books, including *Escape the Coming Night* (Revelation), *The Handwriting on the Wall* (Daniel), *Overcoming Loneliness, God in You* (Holy Spirit), *When Your World Falls Apart, My Heart's Desire, 31 Days to Happiness—Searching for Heaven on Earth, Captured by Grace, What in the World Is Going On?, The Coming Economic Armageddon, I Never Thought I'd See the Day!, What Are You Afraid Of?, Agents of the Apocalypse, RESET—Ten Steps to Spiritual Renewal, Ten Questions Christians Are Asking,* and *A Life Beyond Amazing.*

How to Use This
Study Guide

The purpose of this Turning Point study guide is to reinforce Dr. David Jeremiah's dynamic, in-depth teaching and to aid the reader in applying biblical truth to his or her daily life. This study guide is designed to be used in conjunction with Dr. Jeremiah's *Escape the Coming Night, Volume 2* audio series, but it may also be used by itself for personal or group study.

Structure of the Lessons

Each lesson is based on one of the messages in the *Escape the Coming Night, Volume 2* compact disc series and focuses on specific passages in the Bible. Each lesson is composed of the following elements:

- *Outline*

The outline at the beginning of the lesson gives a clear, concise picture of the topic being studied and provides a helpful framework for readers as they listen to Dr. Jeremiah's teaching.

- *Overview*

The overview summarizes Dr. Jeremiah's teaching on the passage being studied in the lesson. Readers should refer to the Scripture passages in their own Bibles as they study the overview. Unless otherwise indicated, Scripture verses quoted are taken from the New King James Version.

- *Personal and Group Application Questions*

This section contains a variety of questions designed to help readers dig deeper into the lesson and the Scriptures, and to apply the lesson to their daily lives. For Bible study groups or Sunday school classes, these questions will provide a springboard for group discussion and interaction.

- *Did You Know?*

This section presents a fascinating fact, historical note, or insight that adds a point of interest to the preceding lesson.

PERSONAL STUDY

Thank you for selecting *Escape the Coming Night, Volume 2* for your current study. The lessons in this study guide were created to help you gain fresh insights into God's Word and develop new perspectives on topics you may have previously studied. Each lesson is designed to challenge your thinking, and help you grow in your knowledge of Christ. During your study, it is our prayer that you will discover how biblical truth affects every aspect of your life and your relationship with Christ will be strengthened.

When you commit to completing this study guide, try to set apart a time, daily or weekly, to read through the lessons without distraction. Have your Bible nearby when you read the study guide, so you're ready to look up verses if you need to. If you want to use a notebook to write down your thoughts, be sure to have that handy as well. Take your time to think through and answer the questions. If you plan on reading the study guide with a small group, be sure to read ahead and be prepared to take part in the weekly discussions.

LEADER'S GUIDE

Thank you for your commitment to lead a group through *Escape the Coming Night, Volume 2*. Being a leader has its own rewards. You may discover that your walk with the Lord deepens through this experience. Throughout the study guide, your group will explore new topics and review study questions that encourage thought-provoking group discussion.

The lessons in this study guide are suitable for Sunday school classes, small-group studies, elective Bible studies, or home Bible study groups. Each lesson is structured to provoke thought and help you grow in your knowledge and understanding of God. There are multiple components in this section that can help you structure your lessons and discussion time, so make sure you read and consider each one.

Before You Begin

Before you begin each meeting, make sure you and your group are well-versed with the content of the chapter. Every person should have his or her own study guide so they can follow along and write in the study guide if need be. When possible, the study guide should be used with the corresponding compact disc series. You may wish to assign the study guide lesson as homework prior to the meeting of the group and then use the meeting time to listen to the CD and discuss the lesson.

To ensure that everyone has a chance to participate in the discussion, the ideal size for a group is around eight to ten people. If there are more than ten people, try to break up the bigger group into smaller subgroups. Make sure the members are committed to participating each week, as this will help create stability and help you better prepare the structure of the meeting.

At the beginning of the study each week, start the session with a question to challenge group members to think about the issues you will be discussing. The members can answer briefly, but the goal is to have an idea in their mind as you go over the lesson. This allows the group members to become engaged and ready to interact with the group.

After reviewing the lesson, try to initiate a free-flowing discussion. Invite group members to bring questions and insights they may have discovered to the next meeting, especially if they were unsure of the meaning of some parts of the lesson. Be prepared to discuss how biblical truth applies to the world we live in today.

Weekly Preparation

As the group leader, here are a few things you can do to prepare for each meeting:

- Choose whether or not you will play the CD message during your small group session.

  If you decide to play the CD message from Dr. Jeremiah as part of the meeting, you will need to adjust the group time accordingly.

- Make sure you are thoroughly familiar with the material in the lesson.

  Make sure you understand the content of the lesson so you know how to structure group time and you are prepared to lead group discussion.

- Decide, ahead of time, which questions you plan to discuss.

  Depending on how much time you have each week, you may not be able to reflect on every question. Select specific questions which you feel will evoke the best discussion.

- Take prayer requests.

  At the end of your discussion, take prayer requests from your group members and pray for each other.

Structuring the Discussion Time

If you need help in organizing your time when planning your group Bible study, here are two schedules, for sixty minutes and ninety minutes, which can give you a structure for the lesson:

Option 1 (Listen to Audio CD)	60 Minutes	90 Minutes
Welcome: Members arrive and get settled.	N/A	5 minutes
Getting Started Question: Prepares the group for interacting with one another.	Welcome and Getting Started 5 minutes	15 minutes
Message: Listen to the audio CD.	40 minutes	40 minutes
Discussion: Discuss group study questions.	10 minutes	25 minutes
Prayer and Application: Final application for the week and prayer before dismissal.	5 minutes	5 minutes

Option 2 (No Audio CD)	60 Minutes	90 Minutes
Welcome: Members arrive and get settled.	5 minutes	10 minutes
Getting Started Question: Prepares the group for interacting with one another.	10 minutes	10 minutes
Message: Review the lesson.	15 minutes	25 minutes
Discussion: Discuss group study questions.	25 minutes	35 minutes
Prayer and Application: Final application for the week and prayer before dismissal.	5 minutes	10 minutes

As the group leader, it is up to you to keep track of the time and keep things moving along according to your schedule. If your group is having a good discussion, don't feel the need to stop and move on to the next question. Remember, the purpose is to pull together ideas, and share unique insights on the lesson. Make time each week to discuss how to apply these truths to living for Christ today.

The purpose of discussion is for everyone to participate, but don't be concerned if certain group members are more quiet—they may be internally reflecting on the questions and need time to process their ideas before they can share them.

Group Dynamics

Leading a group study can be a rewarding experience for you and your group members—but that doesn't mean there won't be challenges. Certain members may feel uncomfortable discussing topics that they consider very personal, and might be afraid of being called on. Some members might have disagreements on specific issues. To help prevent these scenarios, consider the following ground rules:

- If someone has a question that may seem off topic, suggest that it is discussed at another time, or ask the group if they are okay with addressing that topic.

- If someone asks a question you don't know the answer to, confess that you don't know and move on. If you feel comfortable, invite other group members to give their opinions, or share their comments based on personal experience.

- If you feel like a couple of people are talking much more than others, direct questions to people who may not have shared yet. You could even ask the more dominating members to help draw out the quiet ones.

- When there is a disagreement, encourage the group members to process the matter in love. Invite members from opposing sides to evaluate their opinions and consider the ideas of the other members. Lead the group through Scripture that addresses the topic, and look for common ground.

When issues arise, remind your group to think of Scripture: "Love one another" (John 13:34), "If it is possible, as much as depends on you, live peaceably with all men" (Romans 12:18), and "Be quick to listen, slow to speak and slow to become angry" (James 1:19, NIV).

For Continuing Study

For a complete listing of Dr. Jeremiah's materials for personal and group study call 1-800-947-1993, go online to www.DavidJeremiah.org, or write to Turning Point, P.O. Box 3838, San Diego, CA 92163.

Dr. Jeremiah's *Turning Point* program is currently heard or viewed around the world on radio, television, and the Internet in English. *Momento Decisivo*, the Spanish translation of Dr. Jeremiah's messages, can be heard on radio in every Spanish speaking country in the world. The television broadcast is also broadcast by satellite throughout the Middle East with Arabic subtitles.

Contact Turning Point for radio and television program times and stations in your area, or visit our website at www.DavidJeremiah.org/stationlocator.

ESCAPE THE COMING NIGHT

VOLUME 2

This is the second volume in a four-volume set of study guides on the book of Revelation. Could one book of the Bible be covered in one study guide? Of course—but when the book is filled with as much drama and detail as Revelation, it takes four volumes to do it justice.

The book of Revelation has 22 chapters, and this series of study guides has 43 lessons—an average of almost 2 lessons per chapter of the book. If you are beginning your study with this volume, you would do well to secure volume 1 in the series in order to get the proper background from Revelation 1-3.

That said—what does volume 2 of *Escape the Coming Night* cover? In one sense, the same message as volumes 1, 3, and 4: how to escape the dark night of sin and judgment that is soon to overtake planet earth. *Soon* has been a relative term for nearly 2,000 years. Revelation was probably written in the last decade of the first century —around 95-100 A.D. That means the Church has been anticipating the unfolding of the events of Revelation for over 1,900 years.

As with all things related to End-Times prophecy from Scripture, their unfolding is imminent. That means they could begin at any moment; there is no aspect of biblical End-Times prophecy standing in the way of the next major event on God's prophetic calendar: the Rapture of the Church. Before 1948, that statement could not have been made with equal certainty. While many of the events of the book of Revelation will affect the entire world, the focal point of the book is the nation of Israel and Jerusalem in particular. And prior to 1948, Israel was still in the diaspora—the scattering of Jews to the nations of the world following the Assyrian and Babylonian captivities and the destruction of Jerusalem by Roman armies in A.D. 70. How could events affecting the Jews in Israel take place if the Jews were not in Israel? But in 1948, with the reestablishment of Israel as a homeland for the Jews, the stage was set for the imminent unfolding of the events of the book of Revelation.

And those events begin with the gathering of the Church of Jesus Christ to her Lord at the Rapture—the physical removal of hundreds of millions of people from the face of the earth (1 Thessalonians 4:15-18). One of the last Scriptures studied at the conclusion of volume 1 in this series was the promise made by Jesus Christ to the Laodicean church—emblematic of the current stage of Church history: "I also will keep you from the hour of trial which shall come upon the whole world, to test those who dwell on the earth" (Revelation 3:10). It is that "hour of trial" to which we are introduced in volume 2 of *Escape the Coming Night*.

The "hour of trial" is a seven-year period known as the Tribulation, or "the time of Jacob's trouble" (Jeremiah 30:7). It is a time when Israel is judged for her rejection of her Messiah and when the world is judged for her rebellion against God and His Son. The Church's present posture is to "wait for [God's] Son from heaven, whom He raised from the dead, even Jesus who delivers us from the wrath to come" (1 Thessalonians 1:10).

This volume covers Revelation 4:1-11:14: the beginning of destruction upon the earth, how many are saved and many are martyred during the Tribulation, how God's wrath produces hell on earth, and the appearance of the Beast (the Antichrist, the Man of Sin)—the Satan-empowered world ruler who will ultimately meet Jesus Christ in history's greatest battle, and lose.

A LOOK INTO HEAVEN

Revelation 4:1-11

In this lesson we get our first glimpse of what heaven will be like for the Church.

OUTLINE

It's amazing how many "experts" there are on heaven who have never read one of the most detailed accounts of what it will be like. When a door is opened into an unknown realm, the wise will take notice and learn. Such a door is opened into heaven for all who have eyes to see.

I. **The Rapture of the Church**
   A. The Sequence of Events in the Book of Revelation
   B. The Silence Concerning the Church in Chapters 4-19
   C. The Spirit of God's Transfer From Earth to Heaven
   D. The Similarity Between 4:1-2, 1 Corinthians 15, and 1 Thessalonians 4
   E. The Symbolic Presence of John in Heaven

II. **An Open Door in Heaven**
   A. Seated Upon the Throne Is the Triune God
   B. Surrounding the Throne Is a Rainbow
   C. Sitting Around the Throne Are the Twenty-Four Elders
   D. Sounding Forth From the Throne Are Lightnings and Thunders and Voices
   E. Spread Before the Throne Is a Sea of Glass
   F. Situated in the Midst of the Throne Are the Four Living Creatures
   G. Singing to the One on the Throne Are the Creatures and the Elders

I began my vocational Christian ministry as a youth pastor. If that calling was not challenging enough, my first assignment was to teach the 200 members of the youth group a series on Bible prophecy. I daresay what was true decades ago is still true today: Prophecy is not on the list of the top five things teenagers are most interested in. So I did everything I could think of to make that series of messages appealing to our group.

In one of our Sunday evening youth services I had a group of guys dress up like newspaper boys and break into the service with bags of papers shouting, "EXTRA! EXTRA! READ ALL ABOUT IT! MILLIONS MISSING AROUND THE WORLD!" Someone at that time had published a fictitious newspaper called *The Last News* with headlines and articles about the Rapture of the Church—and copies of that paper were handed out by the newsboys. Of course, if you happen to still be in church the day those papers are passed out for real . . . you're in trouble! But that night at our youth meeting, it served to paint quite a dramatic picture of what will actually take place one day in the future.

In the first volume of this series of study guides on Revelation, we examined the content of Revelation 1-3. Those chapters present a picture of the "Revelator," Jesus Christ, and the Church over the last 2,000 years here on earth. We now turn our attention to the third major part of the outline of Revelation, "the things which will take place after this" (Revelation 1:19), beginning in chapter 4. The scene shifts from earth to heaven as a result of something called the Rapture of the Church.

THE RAPTURE OF THE CHURCH

Although the Rapture is not specifically mentioned in the book of Revelation, it is dearly alluded to in the transition from chapter 3 to chapter 4. It is the only explanation for how and why the venue of Revelation moves from earth to heaven. Several facts help us establish the truth of our assumption.

The Sequence of Events in the Book of Revelation

By the time we reach Revelation 4:1, we have completed the first two segments of the book as outlined in Revelation 1:19: "The things which you have seen" (the view of the glorified Christ; 1:1-18) and "the things which are" (the condition of the seven churches; 1:19-3:22). The second section, "the things which are," extends from the time of the Resurrection of Christ to the return of Christ for His

Church. Sequentially, it is only reasonable to assume that "the things which take place after this" will occur after the age of the Church on earth.

A key Greek phrase links the third part of the outline in 1:19 with the beginning of 4:1. The phrase *meta tauta*, "after these things," occurs in both verses. Revelation 4:1 uses this grammatical link to connect with the third part of the outline in 1:19. And John clearly says that heaven becomes the focal point: "After these things I looked, and behold, a door standing open in heaven" (4:1). After the age of the Church on earth, attention is shifted to heaven.

The Silence Concerning the Church in Chapters 4-19

Revelation 4-19 talks about one thing in its entirety—tribulation on earth. Everything is about judgment that is going to come upon the earth. And here is the most amazing thing about those chapters: Not once is the Church mentioned. If it were on earth during a time of judgment like the coming Great Tribulation it would be mentioned. And if it is not on earth, there is only one place it can be—heaven.

A phrase John uses seven times in chapters 2 and 3 is, "He who has an ear, let him hear what the Spirit says to the churches" (3:6). But when that phrase is used in 13:9, it has changed: "If anyone has an ear, let him hear." The Spirit is no longer speaking to the Church on earth—rather there is an invitation to "anyone" to grasp the message being given. Another important clue is how God is referred to in chapters 4-19. The name by which Christians refer to God is "Father," (Matthew 6:9). But in Revelation 4-19, God is never called "Father." He is referred to as God, Lord, Almighty and other non-personal names by which He was known in the Old Testament. Why? Because His children are no longer addressing Him from earth; they are with Him in heaven.

> *It was said of Jonathan Edwards that he enjoyed walking slowly along garden pathways, praying and meditating. Sometimes he would stop and pick up some little clear stone he found on the ground and look through it at the sunlight. Children thought he was eccentric and would ask him what he was doing. Edwards would simply reply that he was thinking about heaven. One day somebody said the problem with Jonathan Edwards was that he had eternity stamped in his eyeballs.*
>
> David Jeremiah,
> *Jesus' Final Warning*

The Spirit of God's Transfer From Earth to Heaven

In Revelation 2-3, the Holy Spirit was in the midst of the churches on earth. But in Revelation 4:5 we find that the Holy Spirit is now in heaven before the throne of God. Paul says in 2 Thessalonians 2:6-8 that Someone who is now restraining "the lawless one" will be "taken out of the way." The lawless one is obviously the man of sin, or Antichrist, who will have free reign during the Tribulation period. The Restrainer is the Holy Spirit who works through the Church (salt and light) on earth. But when the Holy Spirit, and thereby the Church which He indwells, is taken out of the way, the lawless one is free to do his work.

Revelation 4-19 describes a time when, literally, all hell will break loose upon the earth. That can only happen because the Holy Spirit and the Church have been removed.

The Similarity Between 4:1-2, 1 Corinthians 15, and 1 Thessalonians 4

The Rapture is described in 1 Thessalonians 4 and 1 Corinthians 15. There are three parallels between those passages and Revelation 4:1-2:

1. A Voice: Revelation 4:1; 1 Thessalonians 4:16

   There is the voice of the Lord.

2. A Trumpet: Revelation 4:1; 1 Thessalonians 4:16; 1 Corinthians 15:52

   There is the sounding of the trumpet of God.

3. A Change: Revelation 4:2; 1 Corinthians 15:52-53

   There is a change from physical to spiritual.

The Symbolic Presence of John in Heaven

When John is called to heaven by the Lord ("Come up here," 4:1), that is symbolic of the Church being called to heaven. Just as Jesus loves the whole world but loves the Church in particular, so He loved all the disciples but had a special love for John the apostle ("the disciple whom Jesus loved," John 21:20). When Jesus told Peter, "If I will that [John] remain till I come, what is that to you?" (John 21:22), He was in a sense saying that He was going to give John a view of His Second Coming. John's vision-based presence in heaven is symbolic of the Church's ultimate presence in heaven before the Tribulation.

An Open Door in Heaven

Several things need to be noted before we discover what the Church will encounter in heaven. First, there is an open door (4:1). God wants us to know what is happening in heaven while there is tribulation on earth. Next, through the open door we see worship. That will be the primary activity in heaven. Finally, the key word, or the central element, in chapter 4 is *throne*. It occurs twelve times in chapter 4 and is the element around which everything else in heaven revolves.

Seated Upon the Throne Is the Triune God

The One John saw seated on the throne in verses 2-3 could only be described by comparison to earth's most beautiful objects, like precious stones such as jasper and sardius. These were the first and last stones on the high priest's breastplate (Exodus 28:17-20) and picture the One who is Himself the first and last. Revelation 3:21 has Jesus promising the overcomers the right to sit with Him on the throne; and we know the Spirit is standing before the throne. So the whole Godhead—Father, Son, and Spirit—is found on the throne in heaven.

Surrounding the Throne Is a Rainbow

An emerald green rainbow surrounded the throne John saw. The rainbow hearkens back to God's promise of mercy in Genesis 9:13-16 never to destroy all living things again. While great judgment takes place on the earth during the Tribulation, the Church is safe in heaven, reminded of God's promise of mercy by the emerald-like rainbow circling the throne.

Sitting Around the Throne Are the Twenty-Four Elders

We can tell who the 24 elders are by cross-referencing other portions of Scripture.

1. By the Praise on Their Lips (Revelation 5:8-9)

   In the song they sing, the elders refer to having been redeemed by "the Lamb." That can mean only one thing—the elders are the Church.

2. By the Clothes on Their Bodies (Revelation 19:7-8)

   The elders are "clothed in white robes" (4:4), and 19:7-8 tells us it is the bride of the Lamb that is clothed in white robes of righteousness. The Church is the bride of the Lamb.

3. By the Crowns Upon Their Heads (Revelation 4:4)

   Of the two kinds of crowns mentioned in the Bible, the crowns the elders wore are those which are a victor's crown (*stephanos*), not the crown of a king. The crowns worn by the elders represent the rewards given to the Church at the Judgment Seat of Christ. Again, the elders represent the Church.

Sounding Forth From the Throne Are Lightnings and Thunders and Voices

At Mount Sinai, when the Law was given, there was thunder and lightning and voices. But today, we do not approach a throne of thunder, lightning, and voices—we approach a throne of grace (Hebrews 4:16). But once the Church is removed from the earth, the throne of God once again becomes the source of judgment (verse 5). The day of grace is over, the Church is removed, and judgment again comes from God's throne upon the earth. Numerous times in Revelation 4-19 the manifestation of that judgment is seen (Revelation 8:5; 10:3; 11:19; 16:18).

Spread Before the Throne Is a Sea of Glass

I have not been able to identify precisely what the sea of glass before the throne represents (verse 6), but it is often associated with the throne of God in Scripture. Exodus 24:10 refers to a paved surface of sapphire under the throne of God, and Revelation 21:21 refers to the streets of the heavenly city being paved with pure gold like transparent glass. The sea of glass before the throne appears to be a separator between God and all others—something to keep Him set apart.

> *What a scene! And what an awesome day that will be! When that day comes, I don't want to be empty-handed. I want to have something with which I, too, can honor my Lord and Savior, who redeemed me with His own blood. I want to be able to say to him, "Lord God, I could never repay You for what You have done for me, but I want to lay this crown at Your feet, in token of all You have done for me."*
>
> David Jeremiah,
> *Jesus' Final Warning*

Situated in the Midst of the Throne Are the Four Living Creatures

In and around the throne are four living creatures (verses 6-8) who are, I believe, the same ones Ezekiel saw in his vision of heaven (Ezekiel 1:1, 4; 10:14-17)—cherubim (angels) of heaven, standing guard in the midst of the throne (Genesis 3:24). Their role, as explained in Revelation, chapter 6, is to execute God's judgment upon the earth.

Singing to the One on the Throne Are the Creatures and the Elders

Not only do the four living creatures lead in delivering judgment to earth, they also lead in worship (verses 9-11). And whenever the creatures give glory to God, the elders join in by falling down before the throne to worship God. The focus of the praise around the throne is the "creatorship" of the Son of God. The Father is just about to send judgment upon the earth which, by the end of seven years, will leave the earth destroyed. But the problem is not the earth, it is with sin on the earth. So praise is offered to the One who "created all things" perfectly by His own will.

In the midst of the thunder and lightning and voices, the angels suddenly burst forth with "Holy, holy, holy, Lord God Almighty" and all manner of praise to God. And the elders fall down and cast their crowns before the throne. The rewards we get for serving the Lord are going to get cast right back at the foot of His throne in heaven. Our crowns, our rewards, are all we have in heaven to offer Him, and so we will remove them and cast them before His throne. Because the angels were not redeemed from sin, they cannot worship with the Church by saying, "You are worthy, O Lord." The Church is going to have an intimacy of worship in heaven that only the redeemed can understand.

The best time to prepare for "second-person worship" ("You are worthy, O Lord") in heaven is to begin practicing it now. Find time today to say, "You are worthy, O Lord!"

PERSONAL QUESTIONS

1. In Revelation 4:1, what does the phrase "these things" refer to?

   a. If the Laodicean church (3:14-22) pictures the last stage of Church history, how does that influence the meaning of "these things"?

   b. How does John's invitation to leave earth parallel the Church's leaving earth at the Rapture of the Church? (Revelation 4:1; 1 Thessalonians 4:15-17)

   c. What other instances in Revelation support the argument that the Church will not be present during the Great Tribulation?

   d. Ancient trumpets were used more for signaling and attention-getting than for music. What does that say about the voice in Revelation 4:1?

2. Read 1 Corinthians 15:50-54.

   a. What problem exists when considering human beings going to heaven? (verse 50)

   b. What change will occur to make us fit inhabitants for heaven? (verses 51-53)

   c. How fast will this change take place? (verse 52)

   d. When will it take place? (verse 52b; 1 Thessalonians 4:16)

   e. How does the mention of the "trumpet" in 1 Corinthians 15:52, 1 Thessalonians 4:16, and Revelation 4:1 tie these events together?

GROUP QUESTIONS

1. Discuss the following questions:

   a. Do you think the Church will be present during the Great Tribulation? Why?

   b. What evidence do you have to support your opinion?

   c. List Scripture to support your assessment.

2. Read 1 Thessalonians 4:13-18 and talk about the following questions:

   a. What were Christians in Thessalonica worried about? (verse 13)

   b. What is the general principle regarding death and resurrection for Christians? (verse 14)

   c. What does "the word of the Lord" mean in verse 15? The Old Testament didn't discuss this subject, so how did Paul get this "word of the Lord"? (1 Corinthians 12:14; Galatians 1:15-18)

d. What will be the order of events when Christ returns for His Church? (verses 16-17)

1. First, the Lord will _____

2. Then, the dead in Christ will _____

3. Then, those who are alive will _____

e. What will be eternally true from that point on? (verse 17b)

f. How are these words to be a comfort to any whose believing loved ones have already died? (verse 18)

DID YOU KNOW?

The 24 elders John saw had crowns of gold on their heads. There are five crowns mentioned in the New Testament as rewards for believers: the crown of incorruption (1 Corinthians 9:25-26); crown of life (James 1:12); crown of rejoicing (1 Thessalonians 2:19-20); crown of glory (1 Peter 5:1-4); and the crown of righteousness (2 Timothy 4:8). The crowns will be distributed at the Judgment Seat of Christ following the Rapture (1 Corinthians 3:11-15). The purpose of these crowns is to reward faithfulness in living for Christ, but the crowns will ultimately be laid at the foot of the throne of God in His honor (Revelation 4:10-11).

TITLE DEED TO THE EARTH

Revelation 4 and 5

In this lesson we learn why Jesus Christ is praised in heaven.

OUTLINE

The Lord's Prayer is the most oft-prayed prayer in the world. During the Tribulation period, all of heaven unites in praise as God prepares the answer to the central request of that prayer—that God's kingdom would come, and His will would be done, on earth as it is in heaven.

I. The Identity of the One Who Takes the Scroll
   A. The Lion of the Tribe of Judah
   B. The Root of David
   C. The Lamb Who Was Slain

II. The Locality of the One Who Takes the Scroll

III. The Activity of the One Who Takes the Scroll
   A. He Reclaims Authority Over All the Earth
   B. He Receives the Worship of Heaven

It is well-known among most Bible students that the chapter and verse divisions in our modern Bibles are not part of the original text of Scripture. The book of Revelation, for instance, would have been one long, continuous document with no breaks. There were not even spaces or punctuation marks between sentences! As publishing progressed, however, chapter and verse divisions were inserted to make the study and reading of the Bible easier.

One of the results is that portions of Scripture which are best understood if read together have been broken apart. Such is the case with Revelation 4-5. The first word of chapter 5, "and," ties it to the last verse of chapter 4. Chapter 5 continues the vision of what John saw in heaven when a door was opened and he was called to "come up here" (Revelation 4:1).

We see something in chapter 5 not mentioned in chapter 4: The One on the throne has a scroll, or book, in His hand. The book of Revelation is, indeed, a book about books. There is a book of life, a book of works, a book of testimony—and in the chapter before us is another book which is, in many ways, a key to the unfolding of the rest of Revelation. It is a scroll written on front and back, indicating nothing more could be added, sealed with seven seals (5:1). I agree with those Bible scholars who believe this book is the title deed to planet earth, and that Revelation 5 tells us what the title deed contains and what happens when the seven seals are released.

We said in an earlier lesson that Revelation contains three sets of sevens: seven seals, seven trumpets, and seven bowls. Some have suggested that they unfold consecutively, one after another. But in reality they unfold in a different manner. For instance, the scroll would not have appeared with seven seals along the outside edge. Because John has a Roman scroll in mind, the seals would have been applied as follows: The first portion was written and rolled up, and the first seal applied. The second portion was written, rolled up, and sealed. Then the third portion, and so on, until the seventh seal was applied. In reading the scroll, therefore, that procedure is reversed: Remove the first seal and read the first portion; remove the second seal and read the second portion, and so on until the end.

Another key is to connect the seals with the trumpets and the bowls. To put it simply, the seventh seal is the seven trumpets, and the seventh trumpet is the seven bowls. Therefore, within the seven seals are contained all the seals, trumpets, and bowls—all the judgments of God. And they are all contained in the scroll held in His hand. This book unfolds the story of the Tribulation from beginning to end (chapters 4-19). The venue for chapters 4-5 is heaven, the venue for chapters 6-19 is the earth.

Through the scroll, the title deed to earth, Jesus Christ is going to once again take control of planet earth, a realm which belongs to Him. By the time we get through the seven bowl judgment, we find that "The kingdoms of this world have become the kingdoms of our Lord and of His Christ, and He shall reign forever and ever!" (Revelation 11:15) As the book in the Father's hand is gradually unfolded and judgment is carried out on the earth, it culminates with the earth being delivered into the hands of the King of kings.

I believe the contents of this scroll are the same contents that were sealed up by God in Daniel 12:8-9, sealed "till the time of the end." And the only one in heaven worthy to unseal the book and read its contents becomes the focus of worship in chapter 5. What was sealed up in Daniel's day was unsealed in John's, and the one unsealing the book is "the Lion of the tribe of Judah," Jesus Christ Himself.

THE IDENTITY OF THE ONE WHO TAKES THE SCROLL

There are three names given in Revelation 5:5-7 for the One who takes the book and unfolds its truth.

The Lion of the Tribe of Judah

This title is taken from Genesis 49 when the patriarch Jacob was blessing his sons shortly before his death. He said of Judah, "Judah is a lion's whelp . . . he lies down as a lion; And . . . who shall rouse him? The scepter shall not depart from Judah . . . and to Him shall be the obedience of the people" (Genesis 49:9-10). Jacob's prophecy meant that from the tribe of Judah the Messiah of Israel would come forth. King David was of the tribe of Judah, as was Joseph, Jesus' legal father, and one of Jesus' names while on earth was Son of David (the whole problem

> *I am convinced that in the Great Tribulation the book of Daniel will be the most important reading matter for many people. Imagine some innocent person who doesn't know a great deal about the Word of God, cast into the midst of hell on earth. He says, "Can somebody tell me what's going on?" Someone says, "Let me give you this book. It's the writing of an old sage by the name of Daniel."*
>
> David Jeremiah,
> *The Handwriting on the Wall*

with Saul being the king of Israel was that he was from the tribe of Benjamin, not Judah).

The Root of David

This is a most amazing name given to Jesus. While Jesus was a descendant of David, the text says He was the "Root of David," meaning that it was from Jesus that David came forth. How can that be? Jesus was both the ancestor and the descendant of David. This became an issue in a discussion Jesus had with the Pharisees. Jesus asked them once whose son the Messiah would be. They answered correctly—"the Son of David." Then why, Jesus continued, does David refer to Him as Lord, and quotes for them Psalm 110:1, "The Lord said to my Lord, 'Sit at My right hand, till I make Your enemies Your footstool.'" How could David call his own Son "Lord"? The Pharisees were stumped (Matthew 22:41-46). Jesus referred to the same reality once when He said, "Before Abraham was, I am" (John 8:58). In His humanity He was the "descendant" of David, but in His deity the "ancestor" of David.

The Lamb Who Was Slain

The last of the three titles is the most moving for the believer—the Lamb who was slain. There are four things to know about the Lamb.

1. The Lamb Is Standing

The word *lamb* referring to Christ in Revelation is very important. It brings to mind Isaac asking his father Abraham, "Where is the lamb?" (Genesis 22:7) for the sacrifice. And John the Baptist answering the question centuries later, "Behold! The Lamb of God . . ." (John 1:29) when Jesus appeared. The word *lamb* occurs 28 times in Revelation.

First, the Lamb is standing in the midst of the throne, unusual for a lamb that has been slain. The Lamb standing is indicative of the resurrected Christ—slain but brought back to life. Hebrews 8:1 pictures Christ seated in heaven, but here He has risen and is ready for judgment to begin.

2. The Lamb Is Slain

Though He is standing, the Lamb is still a slain lamb. The marks of Jesus' death will be visible throughout eternity. We will never be allowed to forget the price He paid for our redemption and that it is only through His death that we are able to enter heaven at all.

3. The Lamb Is Strong

The seven horns indicate the strength of the Lamb (5:6), as horns always indicate in Scripture (1 Kings 22:11; Zechariah 1:18).

Though He has been slain, He has not been weakened. And while no real lamb has seven horns, the number seven is the number of fullness and completion. He is totally strong, thoroughly able to execute the judgments recorded in the book.

4. The Lamb Is Searching

The seven eyes represent His all-seeing wisdom. The seven eyes are said to be seven spirits sent out into all the earth, as if to gather information on all that is happening. He is omniscient and omnipresent, both necessary in order to execute a just judgment upon the earth.

A lion and a lamb are a study in contrasts. The Lamb of God was Jesus at His first coming, the Lion of Judah at His second. The Lamb is meek; the Lion is majestic. The Lamb is the Savior; the Lion the Sovereign. The Lamb was judged; the Lion is the Judge. The Lamb brings the grace of God; the Lion the government of God. All of that and more are wrapped up in the Person who holds the scroll while standing in the midst of the throne.

THE LOCALITY OF THE ONE WHO TAKES THE SCROLL

He is worshiped because of where He is—in the midst of the throne of God, in the midst of the 24 elders, in the midst of the four living creatures (Revelation 5:6). He is the center of the worship of heaven.

THE ACTIVITY OF THE ONE WHO TAKES THE SCROLL

Why is the Lamb worthy to be worshiped? For two reasons, because He reclaims authority over all the earth and because all of heaven worships Him.

He Reclaims Authority Over All the Earth

The background for what is happening in Revelation, chapter 5, is Daniel 7:13-14. There, one like the Son of Man, comes to the Ancient of Days and receives "dominion and glory and a kingdom, that all peoples,

> *The kingdom of Jesus Christ is unique. It is a kingdom that has about it the aura of the Godhead. It is filled with deity, a glorious kingdom. There have been times in the history of the world that have been considered the golden ages, but we have never seen anything like what God has in store when He sets up His kingdom.*
>
> David Jeremiah,
> *The Handwriting on the Wall*

nations, and languages should serve Him." In Revelation 5 Jesus is receiving the kingdom from His Father. The Tribulation period is when He moves upon the earth to judge all who are in rebellion against God and to take ownership of earth and establish His rule and reign.

He Receives the Worship of Heaven

Three groups in heaven are pictured worshiping the Lamb.

1. The Worship of the Redeemed

Remember that the elders (5:8) represent the Church, the redeemed. The bowls they hold are filled with the prayers of the saint—the Lord's Prayer, I believe. For it is in the Lord's Prayer that we pray, "Your kingdom come. Your will be done on earth as it is in heaven." That is the prayer that will be ultimately fulfilled by the end of the Tribulation period.

In verses 9-10, the redeemed, the believers, worship the Lamb. The words of their song are in these two verses, praising the Lamb that He is worthy because He has redeemed out of every people those who will reign with Him on earth. Praise His Name!

2. The Worship of the Angels

In verses 11-12 we find new worshipers—angels, "ten thousand times ten thousand, and thousands of thousands." That obviously is not the exact number, but an extravagant way of saying a number beyond measure. The Bible never says how many angels there are in the universe; they are apparently innumerable, never numbered. Can you imagine the sound of that many angels speaking praises of worship to the Lamb?

3. The Worship of the Creatures

Last, the Lamb is worthy of our worship because every creature in the universe worships Him. Verse 13 says that the animal kingdom, even the fish in the sea, break forth in praise to the Lamb. The day is coming when those creatures which we consider to be dumb and beneath us are going to praise the Lamb.

Around the throne of God, closest to the throne, are the redeemed of God who sing a song of praise to God (verses 8-10). Next are the angels who do not sing, but speak words of praise to God (verses 11-12). Finally, every creature on earth will join the redeemed and the angels in speaking forth praises to the Lamb (verse 13). Note that the redeemed are the only ones who offer their praises directly. While the redeemed actually praise God that He has redeemed them, the angels and creatures offer praises for the redemption which the Lamb provided, that is, the redeemed praise God for their redemption, while the angels and the creatures praise God for redemption itself.

Whether the praises are sung (the redeemed) or spoken (the angels and creatures), there is no missing the fact that the central focus of heaven during the Tribulation is a vision of praise to the Lamb who was slain in anticipation of the kingdom He is about to establish on earth—just as it is in heaven.

PERSONAL QUESTIONS

1. Read Daniel 12:1-10.

   a. What time frame is discussed in this passage? (verses 1, 4, 9)

   b. What does the "time of trouble" refer to? (verse 1)

   c. What is Daniel told to do with what he has been shown? (verse 4)

   d. When will this scroll be unsealed? (verses 4, 9)

   e. How does this passage parallel Revelation 5:1-6?

2. Read Revelation 5:5-7.

   a. What are the two titles given for the one who takes the book and unfolds its truth? Describe the meaning behind each.

   b. Explain how Jesus could be both the descendant and ancestor of King David.

   c. Describe the three titles of the Lamb who was slain. What do each represent, and why are they important?

   d. What idea is given to portray what we will be doing in heaven? (verses 13-14)

1. Three series of judgments will be sent from heaven during the Tribulation. By way of overview, identify in a few words the contents of the three series of judgments and discuss them with your group. (Note: the seventh seal is the seven trumpets, and the seventh trumpet is the seventh bowl. So all judgments are contained with the seven seals.)

   a. The seven seal judgments (Revelation 6:1-17; 8:1-5)

      1. The first seal (6:1-2)

      2. The second seal (6:3-4)

      3. The third seal (6:5-6)

      4. The fourth seal (6:7-8)

      5. The fifth seal (6:9-11)

      6. The sixth seal (6:12-17)

      7. The seventh seal (8:1-5)

   b. The seven trumpet judgments (Revelation 8:6-9:21; 11:15-19)

      1. The first trumpet (8:7)

      2. The second trumpet (8:8-9)

      3. The third trumpet (8:10-11)

      4. The fourth trumpet (8:12-13)

      5. The fifth trumpet (9:1-12)

6. The sixth trumpet (9:13-21)

7. The seventh trumpet (11:15-19)

c. The seven bowl judgments (Revelation 16:1-21)

1. The first bowl (16:2)

2. The second bowl (16:3)

3. The third bowl (16:4-7)

4. The fourth bowl (16:8-9)

5. The fifth bowl (16:10-11)

6. The sixth bowl (16:12-16)

7. The seventh bowl (16:17-21)

DID YOU KNOW?

Scrolls were made either of papyrus—a reed that grew along the Nile River in Egypt, the pulp of which was pounded together, dried in sheets, then cut into pieces for writing—or leather (dried, scraped animal skins). Strips of papyrus or leather would be glued or sewn together to create a scroll of an adequate length. The long scrolls were wound around a stick or rod to facilitate handling, and rolled from right to left since Hebrew was read from right to left. The Isaiah scroll discovered near the Dead Sea measured 24 feet in length.

THE FOUR HORSEMEN OF THE APOCALYPSE

Revelation 6:1-8

In this lesson we learn how a fourth of the world's population will be destroyed in the Tribulation.

OUTLINE

A cursory look around our globe reveals some terrifying realities—war, starvation, diseases with no cure, uncontrollable dictators, biological terrorism. Some might think the Tribulation has already begun. In reality, these are just birth pangs of something much worse to come.

I. **The First Seal Opened: The White Horse**

II. **The Second Seal Opened: The Red Horse**

III. **The Third Seal Opened: The Black Horse**

IV. **The Fourth Seal Opened: The Pale Horse**

V. **Conclusion**
   A. The Response of Praise
   B. The Response of Passion
   C. The Response of Personal Evaluation

We have arrived in our study at Revelation 6—the place where the real action of the Great Tribulation begins. Chapter 1 contained the things John saw, chapters 2-3 the things which are, and chapters 4-5 the setting of the throne of God in heaven from which the judgments of the Tribulation will proceed. Held in the hand of the One on the throne is a scroll which is taken by the Lamb who was slain (5:7). That scroll contains seven seals, the seventh of which contains seven trumpets, the seventh of which contains seven bowls— judgments all, about to fall upon the earth.

It will take three lessons in our series to cover all of Revelation 6. In this first lesson of the three, we will cover Revelation 6:1-8 and discover the content of the first four seals which are opened by Christ. The first four seals consist of four horsemen who are released to ride upon the earth, carrying various forms of judgment. In our day, the relevance of the horse as a metaphor for judgment is unfamiliar. But in the biblical world, the horse would have been readily understood. For example, Job 39:19-25 is an extended reference to the esteem in which horses were held in the ancient world. In battle, the strength and fearlessness of the horse was respected. The horse was primarily thought of as a weapon of war more than as an agricultural asset or mode of transportation. So the image of four horsemen would bring to mind immediately the idea of warfare and battle to the ancient reader of Revelation.

Four times (6:1, 3, 5, 7) we read the word, "Come!" Most translations have this command directed to John—but he is already there. It seems better to read the word with its alternate meaning, "go" or "proceed," and have it directed to the four horsemen. Therefore, the living creature issuing the command sends each of the four horsemen out of heaven to their mission on earth—"Go!"

THE FIRST SEAL OPENED: THE WHITE HORSE

The white horse (verse 2) in oriental imagery was the picture of a conqueror. Since it is the first horse sent out at the beginning of the Tribulation period, we must discover the purpose and meaning of this first horseman. Because there is a reference to Christ riding a white horse in Revelation 19:11, some believe that Christ Himself must be the rider on this white horse. But there are some differences which make that conclusion strained, at best. Consider the differences:

- Chapter 19, Christ's weapon is a sword; chapter 6, the rider's weapon is a bow with no arrows.
- Chapter 19, Christ wears a crown (a diadem, or kingly crown); chapter 6, the rider wears a stephanzos, a victor's crown of one

going forth to conquer. It could be worn by anyone, whereas the diadem can only be worn by Christ.

- Chapter 19, the white horse signals the end of judgment; chapter 6, the white horse signals the beginning of judgment. It isn't likely that Christ would appear in both places, especially since His Second Coming is the more logical place for Him to appear to put an end to judgment.

These and other disparities between the two riders lead me to believe that the rider of the white horse in Revelation 6 is not Christ, but the Antichrist. He carries no arrows because we know he conquers in the name of false peace. He is the prince mentioned in Daniel 9:26 who makes a covenant with Israel to protect the Jews from their enemies. This treaty marks the beginning of the Great Tribulation. The next horseman (verse 4) is allowed to "take peace from the earth," the peace which the first horseman, the Antichrist, has established.

The person represented by the rider on the white horse could be alive in our world today since he will appear at the beginning of the Tribulation as a full-grown man. That means he would have been born 30-50 years prior to his appearance at the beginning of the Tribulation. Many believe the world stage is set for the appearance of such a person, meaning he could be alive at this moment.

THE SECOND SEAL OPENED: THE RED HORSE

It is very clear that the rider on the second horse personifies war; its red color (verses 3-4) speaks clearly of the shedding of blood. War is nothing new to the human race; thousands and thousands of conflicts fill the pages of recorded human history. In the last hundred years alone, two world wars claimed the lives of 42 million people with 50 million more being wounded. Millions more civilians were killed or died in concentration camps. But the wars yet to be fought on planet earth, and the suffering

> *In the restlessness of nations and in the revolution of the masses and in the prospect of catastrophic war, the first thing that will happen is to be the appearance of this great, final dictator, this great, final world-tyrant. He will promise peace and he will bring with him every token of affluence and prosperity; and the nations of the world and the peoples of the earth will flock after him. This is our Fuehrer, this is our great leader, this is our saviour and the hope of the world. He comes riding on a white horse, conquering and to conquer. The entire military and economic and political resources of the world are at his disposal.*
>
> W. A. Criswell

which attends war, will be more devastating than anything in history. The "great sword" the rider holds in his hand is the large sword used by Roman soldiers going into battle—used when nations rise against nations.

You may ask why it is important to know about these four horsemen if, as a Christian, I am going to be absent from the earth during the period of the Tribulation. The reason is that every event casts its shadow before it. That which will take place in the future has its portents in the present. The "wars and rumors of wars" (Matthew 24:6) we hear of today are the foretastes of that which is yet to come—and those foretastes are part of the diet of the world each of us lives in today.

As wars and conflicts increase, the world will become restless for someone to bring peace and unity to our divided and embattled world. And it is in that context that the Antichrist will arise. There will be a thin dividing line between the signs of the appearing of the Antichrist and his actual inauguration as a world leader. Between those two events, the Rapture of the Church will occur. But the Church may be on earth during a significant part of the turmoil leading up to the revealing of the Antichrist. That is why it is important to know the stages of judgment represented by the four horsemen.

THE THIRD SEAL OPENED: THE BLACK HORSE

The color black is often connected with death and starvation, and famine often occurs as a result of war. Scarcity of food and other resources often result in an increase in prices so that enough food to subsist on can consume all of one's daily wages. Verse 6 indicates that a quart of wheat, or three quarts of barley (enough for one day), would cost a denarius (penny), which constituted a day's wage in biblical times. In the Tribulation period, along with the appearance of the Antichrist followed by war, famine will appear, and the globe will be wrenched with hunger because of the inability to secure food. All but the rich will suffer, for their staples, oil and wine, will not be harmed. But the average person will border on starvation.

This setting also plays directly into the hands of the Antichrist. Revelation 13:17 says that "no one may buy or sell except one who has the mark or the name of the Beast, or the number of his name." The Beast will control the world through the world's own hunger. Men and nations will do unusual and unplanned things in order to get food—and unfortunately, individuals will as well. Hunger is a basic human motivation, and the Antichrist will use it to his advantage as a means of moving people to give him allegiance.

We see evidences of the politicization of food distribution in some African countries today. The pathetic and heart-wrenching photos we see of starving children and adults (many of them Christians) make us think in terms of food shortages. In reality, what has sometimes happened is that food supplies have been cut off by warring political factions. As the African proverb has stated for generations, "When elephants battle, the ants get trampled." Using starvation as a means of genocide is a twenty-first century reality in our world. If it is happening today, how much more might it continue at the hand of an evil world ruler?

> *By forcing on mankind more and more legal weapons and at the same time making the world more and more independent economically, technology has brought mankind to such a degree of distress that we are ripe for the deifying of any new Caesar who might succeed in giving the world unity and peace.*
>
> Arnold Toynbee

THE FOURTH SEAL OPENED: THE PALE HORSE

The three previous horses each had one rider only. Now John looks and sees that the fourth horse has a rider with another person following (verses 7-8). Death is the rider with Hades following close behind. Death and Hades are mentioned three times in Revelation. Christ has the keys to death and Hades in 1:18, and 20:14 says that death and Hades will be cast into hell. But 20:13 tells us a little more about them. They will be judged one day, following the Tribulation during which they have reigned. They will be judged, "each one according to his works." Found guilty, they will be cast into hell.

After the Antichrist's brief treaty of peace comes war, and after war comes famine, and after famine comes death and Hades. They are armed with the sword, hunger, pestilence (plagues), and wild beasts. These are the four judgments the Lord said he would send in Ezekiel 14:21. In our day, we have seen war and famine wreak havoc on our world, and we are now in the process of seeing pestilence and beasts and plague do the same. Pestilence is a word for "epidemic." The greatest epidemic the world has ever known, AIDS, will kill more people in the world than all previous epidemics combined. Because the incubation period for the HIV virus can be up to ten years, many people are already infected with AIDS (HIV-positive) who do not even know it. As a result, they continue to spread the disease to others. Because AIDS is spread primarily through sexual contact, many people who know they are HIV-positive are unwilling to take necessary steps to protect others from the disease they carry. Children in the wombs of their infected mothers are being born with the disease. Blood supplies are becoming tainted, increasing the risk for surgical patients to become infected. Medical workers can become accidentally infected by contact with tainted blood. The specter of this disease gets more ghastly with each new report and assessment—and still no cure has been found.

Diseases are also spread by "beasts" of the earth—which could be anything from rats, which can carry as many as 35 known diseases, to disease-resistant microorganisms spread by birds and animals which are shipped or which migrate from one country to another. In past decades and centuries, diseases could be contained in their country of origin fairly easily. But today, a person can contract an animal-borne disease in one country (e.g., AIDS or the Ebola virus which both originated in animal populations in Africa) and arrive by airplane in another country in a matter of hours—and be "lost" among the population.

It is not difficult to imagine that "death" and "Hades" will account for 25 percent of the world's population being killed during the Tribulation (6:8).

CONCLUSION

The Response of Praise

Neither is it difficult to see why praise and worship are the central focus of chapters 4 and 5 of Revelation. Why? Because those who know the Lord Jesus Christ as Savior and Lord will be worshiping Him in heaven while the events of Revelation 6-19 are unfolding on the earth. If being excluded from the fourth of the world's population killed by war, hunger, disease, and the beasts of the earth isn't a reason to praise, I don't know what is.

The Response of Passion

But there is another response we should have. It would be selfish and self-centered for us to be concerned only about saving ourselves. If there is any "neighbor" whom we are to love as we love ourselves, we must warn them of what is coming upon the earth. If we really believe the messages of the four horsemen, we will tell anyone and everyone how they can be spared from the torment of the Tribulation.

The Response of Personal Evaluation

Which brings us to the necessary question, where will you be when Revelation 6 begins to unfold on the earth? Don't wait another minute before making sure that when the trumpet of the Lord sounds, you will leave this earth at the Rapture. After that trumpet, after the Church is gone, it will be too late to reconsider.

PERSONAL QUESTIONS

1. Read Matthew 24:3-15.

   a. What question do the disciples have for Jesus? (verse 3b)

   b. How does verse 5 parallel the notion of an Antichrist coming into the world?

   c. Which of the four horsemen in Revelation 6:1-8 could fulfill the sign Jesus mentions in verses 6-7a?

   d. What is the parallel between verse 7b and the horseman in Revelation 6:5-6?

   e. What does verse 9 suggest about when these events will begin— that is, the relation of these events to the rapture of believers?

f. What is characteristic of birth pangs? That is, do they begin slowly and gradually increase or arrive suddenly with full intensity? What does this suggest as to the timing of these events in relationship to the Rapture?

2. Read Matthew 24:32-35.

   a. What sign is evident on a fig tree with regard to the approach of summer? (verse 32)

   b. What should the disciples of Jesus learn from this parable with regard to the end of the age? (verse 33)

   c. What generation did Jesus refer to in verse 34—the generation to which He was speaking or the generation that sees the beginning of the signs He has described?

   d. How certain can we be that the signs (including the four horsemen of Revelation 6) will come to pass? (verse 35)

GROUP QUESTIONS

1. Read Revelation 6:1-8 and discuss the following questions: What do each of the horses and riders personify? What event does each bring to the world? Explain your reasoning for each answer.

    a. The rider on the white horse (verse 2)

    b. The rider on the red horse (verse 4)

    c. The rider on the black horse (verses 5-6)

    d. The rider on the pale horse (verse 8)

    e. What did horses signify in the ancient world? Using that definition, what would the image of four horsemen bring to mind?

2. What evidence do you see in our world today that might be signs of the presence of these four horsemen?

   a. The rider on the white horse (verse 2)

   b. The rider on the red horse (verse 4)

   c. The rider on the black horse (verses 5-6)

   d. The rider on the pale horse (verse 8)

3. Why is it important to study the four horsemen when, as Christians, we will not be present for the Great Tribulation?

   a. What is our calling as we await the Great Tribulation?

DID YOU KNOW?

The four horsemen of the apocalypse, described in Revelation 6:1-8, have become cultural icons and models through the centuries. Their title has been applied to characters in computer games, rock bands, rock songs, NASA scientists during the Apollo era, Supreme Court justices during the New Deal era of Franklin Roosevelt, a group of atheist scientists, professional wrestlers, and a group of computer scientists. The most well-known group were the four members of the backfield on the Notre Dame University football team, coached by the legendary Knute Rockne, in 1924. All are examples of how the truth of Scripture can be diluted by cultural misuse.

THE SOULS UNDER THE ALTAR

Revelation 6:9-11

In this lesson we discover part of God's plan for His chosen people during the Tribulation.

OUTLINE

One of the thorniest theological—and practical—problems the apostle Paul had to deal with in the Early Church was Israel. If they were God's chosen people, why weren't they being saved? Part of the answer to that question is found in the events of the Great Tribulation.

I. **The Context of Their Martyrdom**

II. **The Cause of Their Martyrdom**

III. **The Consequences of Their Martyrdom**

IV. **The Cry of Their Martyrdom**

V. **The Comfort of Their Martyrdom**
   A. They Are Given a Refuge
   B. They Are Given a Rest
   C. They Are Given a Robe

VI. **The Conclusion of Their Martyrdom**
   A. God Has a Plan That Includes Each Detail
   B. God Has a Purpose That Explains Each Delay
   C. God Has a Program That Extends to Each Dispensation

The ancient church father Tertullian said, "The blood of the martyrs is the seed of the church." From the earliest pages of the Old Testament to the book of Revelation, Satan has attacked the people of God. Pharaoh in Egypt, Haman in Persia, Antiochus in second-century B.C. Palestine, Herod in Jesus' day, Jewish leaders in Stephen's day, a different Herod in James' day. And on and on throughout Church history, especially in the days of the Roman Empire, as we have already studied in earlier lessons.

And what about God's chosen people, the Jews? Satan's fury was unleashed against them in full force through Hitler in Germany so that six million perished. It is estimated that by the end of World War II the number of Jews remaining worldwide was less than the number coming out of Egypt in the Exodus.

The fifth seal opened by Christ in heaven is a seal which shows the result of intense persecution of those who stand for the Word of God during the Tribulation. Since all believers were raptured at the beginning of the Tribulation, these souls represent those who are slain "for the word of God and for the testimony which they held" (6:9). We do not see the persecution itself in the fifth seal—only the results of it. As John looks under the altar in heaven he sees the souls who have been martyred for Christ's sake.

THE CONTEXT OF THEIR MARTYRDOM

Primary in our study is the identification of the martyrs of verse 9. Who are they? When and by who were they killed?

As we have already noted, these are saints who became believers during the Tribulation. The Church has been raptured already, and these are part of the unsaved population left on earth. But their persecutors apparently are still alive since they call upon the Lord for vengeance on those who killed them (verse 10). Therefore, they must have been killed during the Tribulation by non-believers still alive on earth.

We must note at this point in our developing understanding of the Tribulation period that God will deal intensely with Israel during those days. The apostle Paul has indicated in Romans 11:25-26 that a partial spiritual blindness has afflicted Israel and will remain in place until "the fullness of the Gentiles has come in." When is that? When the Rapture occurs—when God's salvation from the nations is complete. But after that (i.e., during the Tribulation) God will turn His attention to His chosen people, the Jews. Many Jews will turn to God and reject the Antichrist; and as a result, many will be martyred for their faith. Because of God's turning His attention to His people during the Tribulation, we can assume that the martyred souls under the altar are Jewish Christians.

How do they become Christians during the Tribulation? Revelation 11 teaches us that God sends two witnesses to earth to preach the Gospel, and Revelation 7 mentions 144,000 Jews who will be "sealed" for God's service during this period. In addition, there will be millions of copies of the Bible, books, tracts, and other literature left behind on earth after the Rapture. Through various means, God will provide a witness for the Gospel to those who are left behind after the Rapture. But those who do place their faith in Christ will pay a heavy price for doing so (Zechariah 13:8-9; Matthew 24:8-10; Revelation 12:11).

THE CAUSE OF THEIR MARTYRDOM

Those martyred during the Tribulation are killed for exactly the same reason the apostle John was exiled to Patmos: for their testimony and faithfulness to the Word of God (6:9). Remember the Holy Spirit has been removed from the world at this time (2 Thessalonians 2:6-7), and so the carnal and evil desires of unsaved mankind will run free. Persecution will be as common in that day as it is uncommon in our own. The absence of the Holy Spirit restraining evil is the difference.

Revelation 19:19-21 warns that all who refuse to receive the mark of the Beast (666) will suffer the wrath of the Antichrist. And their testimony refers to the word of judgment they will preach after becoming believers. When they read the Bible and other books about the End Times and realize that God's final judgment is coming upon the earth, new believers will preach to everyone on earth to repent in light of God's coming judgment of all mankind. For that testimony, they will be killed by the Antichrist—

> ...whenever there is a true prophet of God, he will preach judgment. These modern so-called ministers of God speak all things nice. ... There is not any hell and there is not any devil and there is not any judgment of God. ... So we stand up and we speak of the love of Jesus, and we speak of peace, and we speak of all things pretty and beautiful. But remember... the same book that tells us about the good, tells us about the bad. The same revelation that speaks to us about heaven, speaks about hell.
>
> W. A. Criswell

but their souls will be saved by God. The Jewish believers saved during that period will be like the prophets of old declaring God's Word to their own people. Thousands of Isaiahs, Jeremiahs, Jonahs, Ezekiels, and Pauls will be running to and fro over the earth warning their people of judgment.

THE CONSEQUENCES OF THEIR MARTYRDOM

As do many pictures in the book of Revelation, verse 9 has its roots in the Old Testament. Leviticus 4:7 says that the blood of a sacrificial bull was to be poured out "at the base of the altar." And here we find the souls of those martyred for Jesus in the Tribulation under the altar in heaven. Dr. Barnhouse points out that, "We are not to think that John had a vision of an altar with souls peeping out from underneath. The whole teaching of the Old Testament is that the altar was the place of the sacrifice of blood. To be 'under the altar' is to be covered in the sight of God by that merit which Jesus Christ provided in dying on the cross. It is a figure that speaks of justification . . . These martyred witnesses are covered by the work of the Lord Jesus Christ."[1] So they are saved, under the blood, and protected in heaven.

THE CRY OF THEIR MARTYRDOM

It is important to note the difference between the cry of these martyrs (verse 10) and the cry of the Church's first martyr, Stephen (Acts 7:60). Stephen, following the lead of the Lord Jesus, asked God not to hold his persecutors' sins against them. But these Tribulation martyrs want justice—they call out to God for vengeance! We are told in the Church age never to seek vengeance but to leave such matters to the Lord (Romans 12:19). But the Church age ends the age of grace—the Tribulation is the period of the judgment of God. Therefore, the martyred saints are justified in calling out for justice upon those who have murdered the saints of God.

It's amazing that, when they address God, the martyrs don't call Him by the normal word for *Lord*. Instead they call God *Despotes*, the word from which we get *despot*, a ruler with absolute power. These martyrs call out to the one with absolute and sovereign power to avenge their deaths.

Surely, even in this age of grace, every believer has wanted to cry out to the *Despotes* of this universe and ask "How long?" before all the suffering and sin and pain and abortion and AIDS and crime and drugs and all the rest are done away with. All creation groans with the desire to be set free from that which only God has the sovereign authority to avenge.

THE COMFORT OF THEIR MARTYRDOM

The Lord's answer to their cry for vengeance is to give them a white robe of righteousness and a word of comfort (verse 11). They are to rest for a while longer as He will set the balances right all at one time. "The cup of iniquity on earth is not quite full," says the Lord. "There are more of your brethren yet to join you whom I will avenge along with you."

God's heart of compassion is evident toward these martyrs in three ways.

They Are Given a Refuge

We have seen that they are under the altar, meaning they are covered by the blood of God's sacrifice, Jesus Christ. Shielded by the blood of Christ is the safest place anyone can be. The Lord is a strong tower in whom the righteous are safe (Proverbs 18:10).

They Are Given a Rest

The rest which the Lord assigns to the martyrs is echoed later in Revelation: "Blessed are the dead who die in the Lord . . . that they may rest from their labors" (Revelation 14:13). How sweet the invitation to rest would be to those brought out of the Tribulation.

They Are Given a Robe

The Lord went around and gave a white robe "to each of them." The impression is that they were personally given their robe. We have to ask what kind of robes souls wear. The martyrs are not there in their resurrected bodies; rather, they are there as souls. Tribulation saints will not be resurrected until the end of the Tribulation (Revelation 20:5). Dr. John Walvoord's opinion here is helpful—that the Tribulation saints are accorded some type of temporary body in heaven for the short time between their death and the possession of their resurrected bodies.[2] On this temporary body they are able to wear their white robes.

THE CONCLUSION OF THEIR MARTYRDOM

We can draw three applications from these three brief verses about martyred Jewish believers during the Tribulation (verses 9-11).

God Has a Plan That Includes Each Detail

From this passage we take great comfort in thinking about our own physical death should we die before the Lord returns. Some people suggest a doctrine called "soul sleep," meaning the soul of

> *As I write this, I long for everyone to give their hearts to Christ now, when it is comparatively easy to be a Christian. During the Tribulation, the fate of believers will be worse than what happened in the Nazi prison camps during World War II.*
>
> David Jeremiah,
> *Escape the Coming Night*

a person is not animated between the time of death and the beginning of eternal heaven. But that certainly was not the case with the martyred Tribulation saints. They were alive and well, under the blood, conversing with the Lord in heaven! Two things are taught clearly regarding the death of believers and the return of the Lord. When the Lord returns the saints rise from the grave (1 Thessalonians 4:14-16) and they return with Him (1 Thessalonians 3:13b). The only way this can happen is for the body and soul to be separate after death. So the body "sleeps" in the grave, but the soul is alive and returns with the Lord to be reunited with a resurrected body. To be "absent from the body is to be present with the Lord" (2 Corinthians 5:8). God has covered every detail of our future.

God Has a Purpose That Explains Each Delay

What appears to us to be delays in God's deliverance is always explained by His greater purposes which are at work. The martyrs who cried out for vengeance against their persecutors discovered that God had a purpose in His delay. We think God is uncaring or unconcerned or unjust or unable when He doesn't respond to our need right away. But He is none of those things. Rather, He is a God who is working out His purposes on His timetable. In the case of the martyrs, justice would be carried out but at the perfect time. Another group of Jewish martyrs would be received by heaven later in the Tribulation. His plan covers every detail and explains every delay.

God Has a Program That Extends to Each Dispensation

I hear people say, regarding the last days, "The day of salvation is just about over." But it isn't. God's grace extends to every period of man's presence on earth—even the Great Tribulation. I remember being taught in seminary how God's grace is at work in every period of God's economy with man on earth. God is always seeking and calling and extending the offer of salvation. And in the Tribulation there will be untold thousands who will receive His offer of grace and be saved.

The period of God's working with Israel as a nation doesn't officially begin until the Tribulation—though many Jews are being drawn to Christ in our present day. (Remember: Israel's blindness is only partial; see Romans 11:25.) But the day will come when He will pour out His grace upon His chosen people, and many will see their Messiah Jesus. What a joy to know that God has a program which ensures that His grace extends to every age.

In anticipation of the outpouring of grace which will come to Israel in the Tribulation, "pray for the peace of Jerusalem" today (Psalm 122:6).

Notes

1. Donald Grey Barnhouse, *Revelation, An Expository Commentary* (Grand Rapids: Zondervan, 1971), 134.

2. John F. Walvoord, *The Revelation of Jesus Christ* (Chicago: Moody Press, 1966), 134-135.

1. What "reward" was given to those martyred during the Tribulation who were seen "under the altar"? (Revelation 6:11)

   a. What did the white robes signify? (Revelation 7:13-14)

   b. What did the color white signify in Isaiah 1:18?

   c. What did white signify for some of the believers in the church at Sardis? (Revelation 3:4-5)

   d. How is white a symbol of clear, undefiled conscience? (Revelation 3:18)

   e. Why is white (insofar as it relates to purity) the only color of the robes in heaven? (Revelation 7:9; 19:14)

   f. What symbolism is implied by something washed in blood coming out white? (Revelation 7:14)

2. Read Acts 7:54-8:1.

   a. Who was the first martyr of the Christian Church? (verses 59-60)

   b. Who participated in that stoning? (verse 1; see Acts 13:9)

   c. What followed that first killing of a Christian in Jerusalem? (verse 1)

   d. How likely is it that a mob mentality will exist during the Tribulation against Christians?

3. When new converts during the Tribulation are killed, when will they be resurrected since the Rapture has already taken place? (Revelation 20:4-5)

GROUP QUESTIONS

1. Read Hebrews 11:32-40 and talk about the following questions:

   a. Why were some of the Old Testament saints mentioned in verse 35 willing to be tortured and martyred?

   b. Describe the various kinds of suffering these saints endured for the sake of their faith. (verses 36-38)

   c. What did they not receive in their lifetime? (verse 39; see Hebrews 11:13)

   d. With what promise did they die? (verse 40)

   e. What must every believer in God remember during his lifetime? (Hebrews 11:13b)

   f. What has God prepared for those in all eras, especially those who suffer for His Name? (Hebrews 11:16)

2. Discuss the following questions:

   a. What persecutions can you think of that are going on against Christians today?

b. What persecutions do Jews endure today?

c. Talk about some of the persecution suffered by Jews in history. Why do they have such a history of hatred against them?

d. How can we, as Christians, support our brothers and sisters in Christ around the world?

e. How can we, as Christians, support God's chosen people (the Jews)?

DID YOU KNOW?

The most famous book about Christian martyrs in Church history was written by an Englishman named John Foxe and published in 1563—the largest publishing project in England up to that time. Traditionally referred to as *Foxe's Book of Martyrs*, the book's primary title was *Actes and Monuments of these Latter and Perillous Days, Touching Matters of the Church*. The book was updated and enlarged a number of times. It focused primarily on the martyrdom of dissenters and Protestants in England—people like William Tyndale, Nicholas Ridley, and Hugh Latimer. The book is filled with woodcuts depicting the horrific deaths of those who died for the sake of Christ.

WHEN THE WHOLE WORLD TREMBLES

Revelation 6:12-17

*In this lesson we are introduced to the judgments
of the second half of the Great Tribulation.*

OUTLINE

Many first-time mothers think the pain of their pre-birth labor
could not possibly get any worse—until the actual delivery takes
place! The judgments of the first half of the Tribulation period are
like that—mild in comparison to what follows.

I. **The Shaking of the Earth**

II. **The Darkening of the Sky**

III. **The Falling of the Stars**

IV. **The Rolling Back of the Heavens**

V. **The Moving of the Mountains and the Islands**

VI. **The Cry of the Wicked**
   A. Sin's Horror
   B. Sin's Hiding
   C. Sin's Hardness

Everyone in the world today is familiar with earthquakes. The dawn of the twenty-first century has seen massive earthquakes in El Salvador, Turkey, and India which resulted in the loss of tens of thousands of lives. While earthquakes have taken place throughout history, their frequency and severity is on the increase.

It should come as no surprise, then, that when we read of the opening of the sixth seal we find the whole world shaken by a great earthquake. While there has never been a single earthquake of global proportions, with what we are learning about the coming Great Tribulation, it is not difficult to imagine one taking place in those days. The first seal reveals a coming world dictator; the second, war; the third, famine and death; and the fourth, death and Hades. The fifth seal revealed the results of mass persecution and murder of the saints of God during the Tribulation. When the sixth seal is removed from earth's title deed, the earth is shaken by a massive earthquake and other natural calamities which cause people all over the world to cry out in terror (6:16-17).

It is probable that with the opening of the sixth seal we move into what is specifically known as the Great Tribulation—the last three-and-a-half years of the seven year period of judgment on the earth. Verse 17 has people on earth saying, "The great day of His wrath has come," indicating an awareness even by the unsaved that God is judging the earth. As we move from the sixth to the seventh seal, which is the seven trumpet judgments, the judgment intensifies to a level not seen in the first five seals. It's hard to imagine it could get worse, but it does. Combining the sixth seal with Matthew 24 and Daniel 9, we arrive at the end of the first half of the Tribulation.

Many people have taken the events of the sixth seal symbolically, suggesting that they represent turmoil at a political, governmental, and societal level on the earth. I don't believe, however, that any amount of societal upheaval could result in the reactions of terror, panic, and fear we see as a response (6:15-17), especially when the "kings" themselves are part of the panic. I believe we are reading about things that will take place literally in those days—and there are five of them in number.

THE SHAKING OF THE EARTH

Jesus Himself said there would be "earthquakes in various places" in the End Times (Matthew 24:7; Mark 13:8; Luke 21:11). And He wasn't the first. The Old Testament prophets predicted the same thing

(Ezekiel 38:19; Joel 2:10; Amos 8:8; Haggai 2:6). The prophets and the Prophet said God's judgment would be accompanied by earthquakes (verse 12). The shaking of the earth has often accompanied great movements of God in history. The earth shook when Moses received the Law (Exodus 19:18); when Jesus died on the cross (Matthew 27:51); and at the Resurrection (Matthew 28:2). Given the history of predictions or earthquakes and occurrence of earthquakes, it is reasonable to expect the earthquake of the sixth seal to be a literal one.

Proportionally speaking, very few people on earth have ever been through a truly massive earthquake. Living in Southern California, I remember when a 7.6 earthquake shook Mexico City. The epicenter of that quake was 250 miles from the heart of Mexico City. However, because the city was built on an ancient lake bed and not on solid rock, the seismic waves were amplified many times by the time they hit the city. Engineers determined that the buildings were subjected to a force of "one G"—acceleration at the rate of 32 feet per second—for approximately one minute! In non-technical terms, it was as if the buildings in Mexico City were turned parallel to the ground and held there while gravity tore at their foundations. The result was that more than 10,000 people lost their lives in that single earthquake.[1]

That's what happens when the earth shakes in one tiny spot on the surface of the earth. Imagine what it will be like when one earthquake shakes the entire earth.

THE DARKENING OF THE SKY

The darkening of the sun is not a new phenomenon either. It happened during the plagues on Egypt, at Mount Sinai, and at the crucifixion of Jesus. And the prophets included such a thing in their predictions of the End Times (Joel 2:30-31; Zephaniah 1:15; Isaiah 13:9-10; Ezekiel 32:7). Jesus also said the sun would be darkened in association with the Tribulation (Mark 13:24). Such a phenomenon will totally disrupt life on planet earth if it occurs over an extended time—a black sun and a blood-red moon (6:12).

> When the Surgeon General of the United States first issued dire warnings that smoking increased the possibilities of cancer, he wasn't very popular. But he saved lives. I once read about a man who was so concerned from the newspaper articles about the dangers of smoking that he decided to give up the newspaper. Many today are like that with the Bible—just cancel it.
>
> David Jeremiah,
> *Escape the Coming Night*

I have noticed since moving from the Midwest to Southern California that sunlight has an effect on people's moods. People where I live are so used to constant sunshine that they are going to suffer terribly during these days of darkness. I have a pastor friend in Alaska who has to send his wife to stay with relatives for a month or more during the days when there is almost total darkness. Her spirit is so affected by the lack of sunlight, she has to leave. The contrast between darkness and light in Scripture has implications in many realms. Most crime is committed at night. Most depression sets in at night. Satan and sin are associated with darkness. We can only imagine how prolonged darkness across the face of the earth will impact those who are alive in those days. In Pharaoh's case, after only three days he demanded that Moses remove it (Exodus 10:22-24). Since food cannot grow without sunlight, what will happen to the world's food supply?

THE FALLING OF THE STARS

The "stars of heaven" (verse 13) which John saw falling to earth are possibly what we would call today meteors or steroids—not the stars which we see in the heavens on a clear night. Many of those stars are larger than the earth and light years from us. More likely these are falling or shooting stars which will pummel the earth. While there is no record of asteroids hitting the earth in the manner described by John, scientists have long considered it a possibility.

On the night of November 13, 1833, the earth apparently passed through a meteor shower as the sky was filled with the trails of meteorites burning up in the earth's atmosphere. Many people thought the prophecies of Revelation 6 were beginning to happen and the end of the world was at hand. That obviously wasn't the case, but it provided a brief preview of what the falling stars John saw might be and look like. John says the stars "fell to the earth," so if they are meteorites they would have to be huge in order to pass completely through the earth's atmosphere without burning up as most smaller meteorites do. Could God not arrange for the earth to pass through such an extended bombardment at that exact time?

A shaking earth, a black sun, a red moon, meteors hitting the earth, bodies of water causing untold damage, and tidal waves across the globe. The sixth seal brings increasing calamity to planet earth.

THE ROLLING BACK OF THE HEAVENS

Dr. Henry Morris has written on what may be referred to in this aspect of the sixth seal: "The departing of the heavens as a scroll is more difficult to understand. There seems to be two possibilities.

One is that the clouds of dust will gradually spread across the sky making it appear that the sky is being rolled up. However, the use of the graphic term 'departed' seems to indicate something more spectacular even than this. The other possibility is that the earth's crust, highly unstable ever since the Great Flood, will be so disturbed by the impacting asteroids, the volcanic explosions and the worldwide earthquakes that great segments of it will actually begin to slip and slide over the earth's deep, plastic mantle. Geophysicists for many years have been fascinated with the idea of a continental drift. Although strong evidence has been accumulating against any such phenomenon occurring in the present age, several have published theories of a past naturalistic catastrophe involving what they call 'the earth's shifting crust.' Some such phenomenon may actually be triggered under the judgment of the sixth seal dwarfing the damage occasioned by all the mighty earthquakes of the past. Those who reside in regions above such shifting crustal plates will observe the heavens appearing to move in the opposite direction, and it will seem as if they are being rolled up in a scroll."[2]

THE MOVING OF THE MOUNTAINS AND THE ISLANDS

This is probably tied in to the phenomena Dr. Morris described above. Scientifically, we may not know how to describe what is going to happen in those days. But theologically, even emotionally, we can imagine it better. It is as if God has reached down to planet earth with His hands and is shaking the earth—causing everything that is not "tied down" to come loose. The writer to the Hebrews says the day is coming when God says, "Yet once more I shake not only the earth, but also heaven" (Hebrews 12:26; compare Haggai 2:6).

THE CRY OF THE WICKED

There are three lessons to be drawn from the five cataclysmic events contained in the sixth seal.

Sin's Horror

Sometimes we think that the "powerful people" on earth are not frightened by the things which shake the rest of us. But something so horrible is coming upon planet earth that "the kings of the earth, the great men, the rich men, the commanders, the mighty men, every slave and every free man" will try to hide themselves from the events of those days (6:15). The whole fabric of human society is represented—no one will be exempt from the judgment of God.

> *The greatest prayer meeting the world has ever known now takes place, but like most prayers that have been offered throughout the ages by fallen humanity, these are not addressed in the right way. The Bible says "Whosoever calleth upon the name of the Lord shall be saved," but there is no promise made to those who call upon the rocks and the mountains.*
>
> Donald G. Barnhouse

There seems to be an intuitive fear expressed by those who do not even profess to know God that what is happening is coming from the hand of God Himself: "For the great day of His wrath has come, and who is able to stand?" (6:17) The events of the sixth seal are God's response to the horror of sin. No human being can argue with God when they see His divine displeasure at work.

Sin's Hiding

The human instinct is to hide when we are confronted with sin. Whether it's a child who's been caught with a hand in the cookie jar, or an adult being confronted with rebellion against God, we seek to hide ourselves from holiness. Nobody sins in the open. It always takes place in solitude or behind closed doors or under the cover of darkness. Adam and Eve hid from God in the Garden of Eden and we, their descendants, have been doing likewise ever since. Sin makes us hide. During the Great Tribulation people will hide themselves any way they can, ostensibly to protect themselves from physical harm, but in reality to protect themselves from the all-seeing eye of God. Thankfully, through Jesus Christ, we no longer have to hide from God because the guilt and shame of our sin has been removed.

Sin's Hardness

Sin so hardens the heart that even when confronted by God, people would rather die than repent and be forgiven. John sees people crying out, praying, in a sense, to the mountains to fall on them and shield them from the presence of God. You would think people who have seen what these people have seen for over three years would fall down on their faces and repent. Instead, they would rather die. We will discover later in our study of Revelation that, toward the end of the Great Tribulation, "the rest of mankind, who were not killed by these plagues, did not repent of the works of their hands . . . And they did not repent of their murders or their sorceries or their sexual immorality or their thefts" (9:20 and 9:21; see also 16:9, 11, 21). Is that amazing? It is because of the way sin hardens the human heart.

The message for us today is not to take lightly God's attitude about our sin. Even though you may be a believer, sin is still sin. Seeing God's response to the sin of the world in the sixth seal should have each of us confessing our sins before God as well (1 John 1:9).

Notes

1. Bruce W. Most, "Waiting for the Shaking," *Amtrak Express* (Feb/March, 1987), 50.
2. Henry Morris, *The Revelation Record* (Wheaton, IL: Tyndale House, 1983), 123.

1. Read Genesis 3:6-8.

   a. After Adam and Eve sinned and their eyes were opened, what did they do when they heard God approaching? (verse 8)

   b. Have you ever had this response? Why?

   c. What is the natural impulse of man when he sins—to hide or to be forthcoming?

   d. How is the reaction of the people in Revelation 6:15-17 similar to Adam and Eve's in the Garden?

   e. What is your normal response to God when you have sinned or otherwise find yourself in a shameful posture?

   f. What is God always willing to do for those who run to Him instead of from Him? (1 John 1:9)

   g. Based on all the information you have learned throughout this study so far, how will you prepare for the coming destruction? Is there anyone in your life that isn't saved, therefore isn't prepared for the Great Tribulation?

2. Do you ever contemplate the "birth pangs" our world is experiencing today? List some examples of them that you have witnessed.

   a. How can these signs encourage you to turn fully to the Lord and put your full hope in Him?

1. Read Romans 8:18-22 and discuss the following questions:

   a. For what has planet earth been waiting for thousands of years—ever since the Garden of Eden? (verse 19)

   b. Based on what you're learning about the End Times, when will the "revealing of the sons of God" take place? (see 1 John 3:1-2)

   c. When was the earth cursed—subjected to bondage? (Genesis 3:17-18)

   d. In what sense might natural disasters like earthquakes be considered "birth pangs" of planet earth? (verse 22)

   e. What might be considered the moment of earth's "delivery"? (2 Peter 3:10-13)

   f. How might the horrendous natural events of Revelation 6:12-14 be considered the most intense of the "birth pangs" prior to the Second Coming of Christ?

   g. Compare the descriptions in Revelation 6:12-14 with the idea of "glorious liberty" in verse 21. As beautiful as the earth is, how much more beautiful do you anticipate it being when it is freed from bondage?

h. How do Christians resolve the tension of stewardship of creation (Genesis 1:28) with the reality that it is on a downward spiral of decay?

2. Discuss the following questions:

   a. What are the five events contained in the sixth seal? Review each one.

   b. What are some examples of each in our world today that show the time could be right around the corner ("birth pangs" of each)?

   c. What are three lessons we can draw from these events? Why are they important?

DID YOU KNOW?

There has been a dramatic increase in the number of seismic (earthquake) recording stations around the world in recent decades. This has led to a great increase in recording earthquakes, the frequency of which has remained relatively stable according to the United States Geological Survey (USGS). The USGS estimates that since 1900 there have been an average of 20 major earthquakes (magnitude 7.0-7.9) and one great earthquake (8.0+) per year. Given the proliferation of mega-cities in seismically active zones of the world, like Mexico City, Tokyo, and Tehran, the potential exists for a single earthquake to kill as many as three million people.

REVIVAL IN THE TRIBULATION

Revelation 7:1-8

In this lesson we meet 144,000 evangelists who turn their world upside down.

OUTLINE

It's easy to think that the Tribulation period is going to be nothing but darkness and horror on earth. But like so many other dark days on planet earth, with God there is always light. In fact, God releases 144,000 points of light to roam the earth and collect the elect for eternity.

I. **The Setting of the Great Revival**

II. **The Sealed Servants of the Great Revival**
   A. What Is the Seal?
   B. Who Are the Sealed?
   C. Why Are They Sealed?

W e touched on this in a previous lesson and will treat it more in depth now: God has a plan for His people Israel. Sometimes we treat the Bible like an anthology of stories and promises from which we pick and choose a verse to cling to. But the Bible must be read more discriminately than that. Not every verse in the Bible is addressed to me as a Gentile believer; some are addressed to God's chosen people alone. The more I see the pages of history turn and the more I turn the pages of Scripture, the more convinced I am that Israel will yet have her day. This lesson is about a revival that will come to God's people before the end of the age.

The Great Tribulation was referred to in the Old Testament as the "time of Jacob's trouble." While it will be a time of purification for Israel, she "shall be saved out of it" (Jeremiah 30:7). Two things will happen to Israel during the Tribulation: Israel will be disciplined for her rejection of the Messiah, Jesus Christ, and Jews will be prepared to receive their Messiah "whom they pierced" (Zechariah 12:10). In Revelation 7 we have the evidence of a great revival which will come to the earth and be centered around the nation of Israel.

THE SETTING OF THE GREAT REVIVAL

Revelation 7 is a parenthetical chapter which comes between the sixth and seventh seal. There is likewise a parenthesis between the sixth and seventh trumpet judgments and the sixth and seventh bowl judgments. They are periods of God's grace in the midst of judgment. The first six seals have been opened, but before the seventh seal is opened (8:1), there is a period during which people on earth are sealed by God against the coming judgment.

In chapter 7 of Revelation there are two visions presented to John. The first one (7:1-8) takes place on earth and concerns 144,000 representatives of a godly remnant from Israel. The second (7:9-17) takes place in heaven and concerns the glory of martyred Gentile saints in heaven. We will study the first vision in this lesson and the second one in the next lesson.

John sees four angels restraining the winds of judgment that are about to blow upon the earth from every direction. The winds of judgment are being held back until the elect from Israel have been gathered in.

THE SEALED SERVANTS OF THE GREAT REVIVAL

It is easy to see what the judgments being restrained by the four winds are destined to accomplish by looking ahead to Revelation 8:6-7: Destruction upon the earth, sea, and trees. Before that can happen the servants of God must be sealed on their foreheads (7:3). What exactly is the seal of God on these Jews?

What Is the Seal?

This is not the first time God has sealed, or protected, people from impending judgment. Think of Noah and his family, Rahab and her family at Jericho, and God's willingness to spare just ten in Sodom if there were that many righteous ones there. And God sealed 7,000 prophets in Elijah's day who had not bowed the knee to Baal, and hundreds of thousands of Hebrew slaves on the night of the Passover in Egypt. God has always protected His remnant when judgment fell upon everyone else.

In Revelation 13 we will read about the seal, or mark of the Beast, 666, without which no one in the Tribulation will be able to buy or sell. Even Satan marks his own. Those who refuse the seal of the Antichrist will be martyred for their faithfulness to God. In Ezekiel 9:3-4, the prophet spoke of a man with an inkhorn who was commanded to "set a mark" upon the foreheads of those who hate wickedness. And then, when the 144,000 surface in Revelation 14, we find they have the "Father's name written on their foreheads" (14:1). They are described as those who would not yield spiritually or morally from their commitment to God (14:4-5).

We don't know exactly what the seal will be. Ephesians 4:30 talks about the seal of the Holy Spirit, and Joel 2 talks about a great outpouring of the Holy Spirit which will occur in Israel in the Day of the Lord. Perhaps the seal is a mighty filling and sealing and anointing of the Spirit by which they are witnesses for Christ during the Tribulation. And what a mighty seal that would be! Consider what it would be like for 144,000 Spirit-anointed Jews suddenly to discover the Messiah. Their witness would be unstoppable. Their appearance might even reflect their Spirit-seal, just as Moses' very face was changed after being with God.

If we compare what happened in the wake of the 12 apostles who were "sealed" with the Holy Spirit at Pentecost, the idea of 144,000 similar Jewish witnesses is staggering. My experience today is that a born-again, filled-with-the-Spirit Jewish believer puts a Gentile believer to shame in his witness for Christ. If 12 Jews turned their world upside down in the first century (Acts 17:6), think what 144,000 could do.

Who Are the Sealed?

> As I read the Bible, when God says "children of Israel," I do not understand Him to mean any but people of Jewish blood, be they Christians or not; and when He speaks of the twelve tribes of the sons of Jacob, and gives the names of the tribes, it is impossible for me to believe that he means the Gentiles, in any sense or degree, whether they be believers or not.
>
> Joseph A. Seiss

Without question, this is the most important and at the same time controversial question in the entire book of Revelation. Before we identify who they are, let's identify who they are not:

1. They Are Not the Same as the Multitudes at the End of This Chapter

Further ahead in this chapter, a great multitude is seen in heaven from every kindred, tribe, and tongue (7:9). It is obvious that these are not the 144,000—they are Gentiles from every nation. I personally believe these are the converts won to Christ by the 144,000 during the Tribulation.

2. They Are Not the Church

The Church is already in heaven, which we established in earlier lessons, represented by the 24 elders. In Revelation 14 we have both the elders and the 144,000 presented as two distinct groups; they are not the same. No error of interpretation is so damaging as substituting the Church for Israel in Scripture. They must be kept separate in order to avoid spiritualizing and allegorizing many parts of Scripture.

3. They Are Not the Seventh-Day Adventists

The Seventh-Day Adventists believe they are the 144,000 of Revelation. They believe that the 144,000 are members of their church who were found faithfully observing the Sabbath when the Lord returns and are raptured to glory. The problem with this is that all Seventh-Day Adventists would have to be Jewish since the 144,000 are plainly Jewish (7:4-8).

4. They Are Not the Jehovah's Witnesses

The original Jehovah's Witnesses believed they were the 144,000. But when their sect grew to more than that number, they changed their theology and called the extras the "overcomers." They try through their works to be promoted into the 144,000 who will be sealed through the Tribulation.

It is a mystery to me why, when a passage is as clear as this one is, people try to reinterpret it to mean something else. The 144,000 are 12,000 Jews from each of the 12 tribes of Israel, just as the text states (7:4-8). The number 12 in Scripture is always associated with Israel. Twelve tribes, 12 stones on the High Priest's breastplate representing the 12 tribes, 12 loaves of showbread in the tabernacle representing the 12 tribes, 12 gates in the New Jerusalem, 12 thrones for the 12 apostles who will judge the 12 tribes. The 12 tribes of Israel did not get "lost" during the exile, a belief known as "British Israelism." Why would the 12 tribes be named specifically in the text if they were lost? There are four notable points in the list of the 12 tribes given in Revelation:

Exception # 1: In this list, Judah is mentioned first though Reuben was the firstborn. He is probably put first because of Jacob's prophecy of his preeminence (Genesis 49:10).

Exception # 2: The son of Jacob named Dan is missing from the list. Dan became an idolater in the Old Testament (Leviticus 24:10-11; Judges 17-18; 1 Kings 12:28-30), which may be why he is excluded. Some even think the Antichrist may be a descendant of the tribe of Dan.

Exception # 3: Levi is listed here, though he is usually unlisted from many lists of the 12 tribes. He is normally unlisted because he received no geographical inheritance. Rather, as the tribe of priests, Levi's inheritance was from all the other tribes. But he is probably included here because the 144,000 are servants of God which Levi definitely was.

Exception # 4: Ephraim is missing. He was not a son of Jacob but of Joseph. He and his brother Manasseh took Joseph's place in the 12 tribes (with the omission of Levi). But here Joseph and Manasseh are listed, but Ephraim is not included. This is one that I don't have a certain explanation for.

Why Are They Sealed?

There are three reasons the 144,000 will be sealed during the Tribulation:

1. They Are Sealed for Protection (Zechariah 13:8-9)

Zechariah suggests that two-thirds of the Jews alive during the Tribulation will be killed. The one-third that survive will come through the fire, refined as silver and gold are. The

144,000 will be like the three young Hebrews who were put in the fiery furnace in Babylon but came through the fire unscathed. Revelation 9:4 says that those who "do not have the seal of God on their foreheads" are the ones who will be harmed. So the 144,000, the sealed by God, will not be touched. They will be protected from the terrible judgments which abound during the Tribulation.

2. They Are Sealed for Power

As we have already learned, these Jews will be empowered to preach the Gospel to their world, and the result will be revival explainable only in terms of the Holy Spirit and His filling. As previously mentioned, I believe the great multitude of the redeemed at the end of this chapter are those who are won to Christ by this multitude of Jewish evangelists. From all over the world non-believers will be converted to Christ and make their way to the heavenly kingdom as a result of the empowered witness of the 144,000.

3. They Are Sealed for Promise

At the end of the Tribulation the Lord Jesus Christ returns to earth to initiate a thousand years of peace and righteousness on earth. Who will populate the earth at the beginning of His kingdom? The ungodly have been judged, leaving only the 144,000 who have been preserved, and any of their converts not martyred for their faith, who will enter the kingdom on earth. The Jewish king, the Son of David, Jesus Christ, will rule over His Jewish brethren at the start of the earthly millennial kingdom. This is the reverse of what happened at His first coming when His own "did not receive Him" (John 1:11). The promised Messiah of Israel will finally rule over God's chosen people.

The 144,000 are sealed by God for protection, power, and promise. A literal kingdom of God is coming upon this earth, a kingdom for which the 144,000

> *I have watched Billy Graham crusades and have been overwhelmed by the hundreds and thousands of people who respond to a simple, straightforward Gospel message. Can you imagine how it will be when those Jewish Billy Grahams begin to preach? Stadiums will not be able to hold the masses. As they leave the sites of these evangelistic rallies, the gestapo of the Antichrist will probably be waiting at the gates, searching for those who have the seal of God.*
>
> David Jeremiah,
> *Escape the Coming Night*

are the building blocks. Even in the midst of unparalleled judgment on earth, the God of mercy reaches down and extends grace and mercy to a remnant of His people that faith may be preserved on the earth. A kingdom must have subjects, and God's grace provides them.

God's grace came before the Flood; it came before Sodom and Gomorrah; it came before Jericho. And most importantly of all, it came before the judgment which we all deserved when Jesus went to the cross in our place. Never is God's grace so clearly seen than at the Cross of Calvary. It is the death of Christ on the cross which allowed grace to be extended in every other time in history—"For God so loved the world . . . ."

And for those times when you think God's grace is not sufficient for you . . . go to Ezekiel 48. In the list of those who will inherit the Millennial Kingdom, Dan is back on the list!

PERSONAL QUESTIONS

1. Answer the following questions from verses in Romans 10-11:

   a. What was Paul's desire for the Jews? (verse 10:1)

   b. What did the Jews of his day have, and what did they lack? (verse 10:2)

   c. What was their fundamental error? (verse 10:3)

   d. Has God rejected the Jews because of their national rejection of Christ? (verses 11:1, 11)

   e. What is the evidence today that Israel has not been rejected by God? (verse 10:5)

   f. Why can't those besides the remnant "see" spiritually today? (verses 11:7-10)

g. What will be the ultimate effect on Israel of salvation coming to the Gentiles? (verse 11:11)

h. Who is the root and who are the branches in Paul's discussion? (verses 11:17-24)

i. What is God's ultimate plan for the Jews? (verses 11:26-27)

j. What is the proof that disobedient people can still be saved? (verse 11:30)

k. What is the attribute of God that allows this? (verses 11:30-32)

l. How do all of these factors tie in with what we know about the Great Revival in Revelation 7:2-8?

GROUP QUESTIONS

1. Discuss the following questions:

   a. Who are the sealed?

   b. Why are they so important?

   c. Why is it important to study them?

   d. What impact do you believe they will have on the world?

   e. Explain what "sealed" means.

   f. Why are they sealed?

2. What was the purpose of the seal mentioned in 1 Kings 21:8 and Esther 3:12; 8:8, 10?

   a. What does the act of sealing accomplish in Daniel 12:4, 9?

   b. What kind of seal did Abraham receive as a sign of his righteousness? (Romans 4:11)

   c. How did believers serve as a seal to the apostle Paul? (1 Corinthians 9:2)

   d. By whom have believers in Christ been sealed? (Ephesians 1:13; 4:30)

   e. What is the purpose of the seal God will one day put on Satan? (Revelation 20:3)

f. Why did God put a mark on Cain after Cain killed his brother Abel? (Genesis 4:15)

g. Who received a mark on their forehead in the city of Jerusalem during the days of apostasy? (Ezekiel 9:4)

h. How do these examples of sealing parallel with the sealed 144,000 studied in this lesson?

DID YOU KNOW?

The only evidence we have of the kind of mark or seal that might be affixed as an identifying mark is found in Ezekiel 9:4: "put a mark [Hebrew *taw*] on the foreheads of the men . . . ." *Taw* is the last letter in the Hebrew alphabet. In ancient Hebrew orthography, the letter *taw* was written in the form of a modern English letter X. So to put a mark (letter *taw*) on the forehead would have been the equivalent of marking the forehead with an X (NIV, note on Ezekiel 9:4).

TRIBULATION HARVEST

Revelation 7:9-17

In this lesson we meet those who are delivered through the Great Tribulation.

OUTLINE

When we find ourselves in trouble, our prayer is usually, "Lord, get me out of here!" We want to be delivered *out of* our affliction. But God's plan is usually not to deliver out of, but to deliver *through*. Believers in the Great Tribulation learn that, even in death, they are delivered.

I. The Status of the Multitude in Heaven

II. The Salvation of the Multitude in Heaven

III. The Safety of the Multitude in Heaven

IV. The Singing of the Multitude in Heaven

V. The Service of the Multitude in Heaven

VI. The Shepherding of the Multitude in Heaven

OVERVIEW

There is a church in Hawaii I have visited on several occasions which reminds me of the passage we will study in this lesson. Located between continents, at the crossroads of the Pacific Ocean, this church has members from "every nation, tribe, people and language" (Revelation 7:9; see also 5:9; 11:9; 13:7; 14:6; 17:15). Many Polynesian ethnic groups are represented along with multiple races from many countries. You feel like you are looking at a snapshot of heaven.

The vision John saw of a "great multitude" in heaven, too large to count, immediately raises the question, "Who are they?" We touched on the answer to that question in our last lesson since they are related to the 144,000, but in this lesson we will identify them further and determine how they came to be in John's vision of heaven.

I find myself in disagreement with a number of commentators on this passage who believe that this vast multitude is the Church of Jesus Christ gathered in heaven. But we have seen that the Church is already in heaven represented by the 24 elders sitting around the throne (Revelation 4). In fact, when John is asked by one of the elders, "Who are these . . . " (7:13), he didn't know. If they had been the Church, he would have recognized them as such. But he had no idea who they were. There are a number of significant differences between the elders in Revelation 4 and the multitude in Revelation 7 which make it impossible for them to be the same people.

It is important to remember that Revelation pictures God's progressive work as people are added to the roll in heaven. They all go into the eternal kingdom together but they have to be kept separate as we identify them in the various places they appear in Revelation. This group in Revelation 7 is a group of (predominately) Gentile believers who have been saved during the Tribulation period as a result (primarily) of the witness of the 144,000 Jewish evangelists (Revelation 7:1-8). The majority of the saints in the Tribulation period will die as martyrs as a result of the persecution of believers by the Antichrist. Therefore, we read in Revelation 7:14 that "these are the ones who come out of the great tribulation, and washed their robes and made them white in the blood of the Lamb."

It is a mistake for us to believe that someday in the future, when the last person who needs to hear the Gospel is preached to, then Christ will return for the Church. That is incorrect. There is not one thing that needs to happen before Christ can return for His Church.

As we have seen, there is a vast multitude of people who are going to be saved after Christ returns for His Church in the Rapture—those who are saved during the Tribulation which takes place after the Church is in heaven. The Gospel will be preached for seven more years after the Church has been raptured.

THE STATUS OF THE MULTITUDE IN HEAVEN

The status of the multitude in heaven is that they are "standing before the throne and before the Lamb." They are standing, as opposed to the Church which is seated, around the throne (the 24 elders in Revelation 4). Their position is one of prominence and power and honor before the throne of Almighty God.

THE SALVATION OF THE MULTITUDE IN HEAVEN

In verses 9, 13, and 14 we learn that the multitude is clothed in white robes which have been made white in the blood of the Lamb. In 6:11 we saw a group who had been martyred for their faith who are told to wait for the rest of their brothers who were to be killed as well. Both those in Revelation 6 and these in chapter 7 are clothed in white robes—the white robes always signifying one of two things: They have either been saved and clothed in the righteousness of Christ, or, as believers, they have clothed themselves in works of righteousness as faithful followers of Christ.

THE SAFETY OF THE MULTITUDE IN HEAVEN

Two things indicate their safety in heaven: palm branches in their hands and God in their midst.

The meaning of the palms (7:9) is not immediately clear from the text, but it becomes clearer from the context of Scripture as a whole. Palms were a part of the celebration of the Feast of Tabernacles when the Jews built small, temporary booths, or huts, to live in during the Feast to remember their deliverance by God from slavery in Egypt. The Feast of Tabernacles was also renewed and celebrated with fervor when the Jews were delivered from trouble such as the Babylonian captivity. These believers who have been rescued from the trouble of the Tribulation appear in heaven, before the throne of God, waving palm branches before the Lord. The palm branches were symbols of celebration and deliverance from trouble.

The image of the palm branches is nowhere pictured better than in Jesus' triumphal entry into Jerusalem on what we now refer to in the Christian calendar as Palm Sunday, the Sunday beginning Passion Week. John 12:12-13 pictures the multitude who went out to meet Jesus as He approached Jerusalem. Waving palm branches in their hands, they "cried out, 'Hosanna! Blessed is He who comes in the name of the Lord! The King of Israel.'" While the Jews thought they were celebrating the end of Roman dominion over Israel, they were indirectly, in the plan of God, celebrating the suffering Servant who was coming to die for their sins. Palms represent joy and gladness in the purposes of God, and for the believers in Revelation 7 the celebration is based on their deliverance to heaven from the Great Tribulation.

As for God dwelling in their midst (verse 15), the text says, "He who sits on the throne will dwell among them." The phrase actually says, "He who sits on the throne shall spread his tent over them." It is the same word used in John 1:14, *skenoo*, which says, "the Word became flesh and dwelt [tabernacled, spread His tent] among us." The tent is an invitation to dwell together, to be protected by being brought into God's protective dwelling place. To come out of the Tribulation and find yourself standing at the door of the tent of God would generate feelings of safety and security to be sure.

THE SINGING OF THE MULTITUDE IN HEAVEN

The multitude is standing before the throne of God saying, "Salvation belongs to our God who sits on the throne, and to the Lamb!" (7:10) They are obviously praising God for their salvation, for having been brought through the Great Tribulation. The commentator and historian William Barclay explains the nature of their salvation experience: "It is not a deliverance which saves a man from trouble but one which brings him triumphantly through trouble. It does not make life easy, but it makes life great. It is not a part of the Christian hope to look for a life in which a man is saved from trouble and distress; the Christian hope is that a man in Christ can endure any kind of trouble and distress, and remain erect all through them, and come out to glory on the other side."

These saints felt the sting of the Tribulation, even the sting of death, but they went through it all and were delivered on the other side. They gave their lives and shed their blood but still experienced deliverance. Just as Christ overcame, they became overcomers as well and are celebrating their deliverance in heaven. Just as He was greeted with shouts of "Hosanna!" when He entered Jerusalem, so He is here greeted by shouts of "Salvation belongs . . . to the Lamb!" (7:10)

THE SERVICE OF THE MULTITUDE IN HEAVEN

We are saved to serve God—even in heaven. Verse 15 indicates that the great multitude saved out of the Tribulation serves Him "day and night in His temple." The reference to "day and night" is simply the Hebrew way of saying, "all the time."

Serving God continually in His temple was a privilege accorded two groups of people in the Old Testament: the Levites and the priests (1 Chronicles 9:33). Gentiles living during the time when the temple was standing in Jerusalem were never allowed to serve there. In fact, they couldn't even enter the inner recesses of the temple itself. A court area called the Court of the Gentiles was as far as they could go—on pain of death. But note the difference with the court in heaven. People from every race and tongue and nation are allowed to serve God in His temple all the time. No barriers or walls keep them out of the temple of God. There is absolute openness and freedom of access to His presence.

Serving God continually, without respect to time, is going to be the chief occupation of all who enter into the heavenly kingdom of God. Those Christians who at this time don't think such a pastime is going to be very much fun, especially for all eternity, have never discovered the joy of serving the Lord on earth. Those who know the greatest joy on earth is serving God can't wait to do it for eternity.

THE SHEPHERDING OF THE MULTITUDE IN HEAVEN

When I read verses 16 and 17, I am reminded of Psalm 23. This multitude of believers is going to be shepherded in heaven by the same Good Shepherd whom David was thinking of in Psalm 23. No hunger, no thirst, no brutal sun bearing down, being led to living waters by which to lie down and rest. This is almost an exact fulfillment of the prophecy of Isaiah 49:10 which God promised to fulfill for His people one day.

Reading the promises of this kind of shepherding in Psalm 23 or Isaiah 49:10 is one thing, but to read it in the context of the Great

Tribulation is another. The Antichrist has been starving these believers, and the waters have been turned to blood (Revelation 16:4). Without the mark of the Beast they haven't been able to buy their food, so they have been forced to find food wherever they could. Many people will probably starve during the Tribulation. Everything they lacked in the Great Tribulation is being given to them by their Shepherd in heaven—along with the promise that they will "neither hunger anymore nor thirst anymore" ever again (7:16). Their Tribulation tears will be wiped away never to be seen again. Words are limited in conveying how complete the care of God will be for those who come through the Great Tribulation, martyrs for their faith.

The very last phrase of chapter 7 is the one most people cling to more than any other: "And God will wipe away every tear from their eyes." The phrase literally means that God will wipe every tear out of their eyes so that nothing is left. He takes the tears out of their eyes so that they cannot weep again. When God wipes away tears then there will be no more tears at all.

But we have to notice something important about the tears which are wiped away—there are tears in heaven, otherwise there wouldn't be any to wipe away. Twice in Revelation God wipes tears away—here and in Revelation 21. In the latter instance, God wipes away all tears following the Great White Throne Judgment when nonbelievers are judged and sent to hell (21:4). When God wipes away tears in Revelation 7, it is at the conclusion of the Tribulation. And, if you remember, what has been taking place in heaven during the Tribulation is the Judgment Seat of Christ for believers. So after each of the judgments—one for believers, one for nonbelievers—tears are wiped away. I believe the saved will weep on both those occasions. First, at the Judgment Seat of Christ, for things we could have done for the Lord and didn't. And second, at the Great White Throne Judgment, for people we could have witnessed to and didn't.

Every believer needs to take stock of those two evaluation points in the future and do now whatever will lessen the tears which may be shed in heaven.

PERSONAL QUESTIONS

1. The multitude discussed were likely saved through the witnessing of the 144,00, but even without the 144,000 Jewish evangelists spreading the Gospel during the Tribulation, there will be millions of copies of the Bible available for people to read. So then, even through the Great Tribulation, there is still no excuse to deny Christ.

   a. How is it possible for a person to be saved just by reading the Bible? (Hebrews 4:12)

   b. How does the Bible discern a person's "thoughts and intents"? (Hebrews 4:12)

   c. Why can the Word of God break through even the most hardened heart? (Jeremiah 23:29)

   d. How can the Word of God cleanse a person of spiritual impurity? (Ephesians 5:26)

   e. Whether it is spoken or written, what is it that results in a person being born again? (1 Peter 1:23)

   f. What adjective is used to describe the "oracles" (words) Moses received on Mount Sinai? What is the implication for its ability to result in change? (Acts 7:38)

1. Discuss the following questions:

   a. Who are the great multitude mentioned in Revelation 7:9?

   b. Who are they not?

   c. Describe them: What are they doing? What do they look like? What are they holding?

   d. Discuss the significance of each of these things.

2. Read Luke 15:1-32 and discuss the following questions:

   a. How do these parables relate to the multitude in Revelation 7:9?

b. What is the theme of all three parables Jesus told?

c. What is the natural response on earth when something that has been lost is found? (verses 6, 9, 24)

d. What does Jesus say is the response in heaven when a lost soul is "found"? (verses 7, 10)

e. How many people getting saved does it take to set off rejoicing in heaven? (verses 7, 10)

f. Why is the degree of rejoicing pictured in Revelation 7:9-12 not surprising? (Compare the "one" in Luke 15:7, 10 with the "multitude" in Revelation 7:9)

g. What connection do you see between Jesus' statement in Luke 15:7 and the older brother in verses 28-30?

h. Based on what you've learned so far, what will have happened to non-Christians in the Tribulation to make them see their need for repentance when previously they didn't?

DID YOU KNOW?

Many will be saved and many lost during the seven-year Tribulation based on their response to the Word of God. When preaching the Word of God in Pisidian Antioch, Paul said to the Jews, "It was necessary that the word of God should be spoken to you first; but since you reject it . . . we turn to the Gentiles." Those Jews were lost because of not believing the Word of God that they heard. Jesus said, "He who does not believe is condemned already, because he has not believed in the name of the only begotten Son of God" (John 3:18). One is not saved or lost based on the presence or absence of sin but on whether or not one has believed and accepted God's provision for sin.

THE SEVENTH SEAL

Revelation 8:1-13

In this lesson we discover the contents of the first four trumpet judgments.

OUTLINE

Some people read about the events of the Tribulation and wonder how God could allow, much less cause, such terrible things to happen to people. If we are offended by the terrible things to come upon the earth, think how much man's sin is an offense to a holy God.

I. **The Silent Pause**

II. **The Silent Preparation**

III. **The Saints' Prayers**

IV. **The Sinners' Punishment**
  A. The First Trumpet: a Third of the Trees and All the Grass
  B. The Second Trumpet: a Third of the Sea Creatures and a Third of the Ships
  C. The Third Trumpet: a Third of the Fresh Water Supply Poisoned
  D. The Fourth Trumpet: a Third of the Sun, Moon, and Stars Darkened

B efore we begin our study in the eighth chapter of Revelation, let's take stock of what we know: The Church of Jesus Christ is no longer on the earth, having been raptured prior to the beginning of the Tribulation. Most of the Jews and Gentiles who come to faith in Christ during the Great Tribulation are being martyred for their faith and are making their way to heaven as well. On earth, the seals are breaking open, and the judgments released by each are taking their toll on the earth.

There was a parenthesis in chapter 7 between the sixth seal (6:12-17) and the seventh seal which we will begin considering in this lesson (8:1). Plagues, wars, scarcity of food, natural disasters, and persecution have filled the earth and left it as a desolate place. But the end is not in sight; more judgments will come as the seventh seal is opened.

When the seventh seal is opened, seven trumpet judgments are released. And when we get to the seventh trumpet judgment, we will find it sounding forth seven bowls of judgment which will be poured out. In other words, the seventh seal has within it the rest of the book of Revelation and the plan of God for planet earth. As we get into the seven trumpet judgments, we find Satan's presence in the man of sin, the Antichrist, becoming increasingly more manifest.

In this lesson, we will study the first four of the seven trumpet judgments with which Revelation 8 is concerned.

THE SILENT PAUSE

That which is about to be unveiled is so serious that it is preceded by a period of silence in heaven. Prior to Revelation 8:1 there has been a cacophony of praise going on in heaven— angels, elders, saints, living creatures singing and shouting praise to God. But all of that noise suddenly ceases, and there is absolute quiet in the heavenly places. This is a foreshadowing of the solemn revelation that is about

> *Before the next series of plagues is described, there is a dramatic pause. The conductor's baton is raised and the orchestra is waiting for his signal to begin the overture . . . How can our limited minds describe silence in heaven? It's like catching your breath before making a ten-meter dive into a cold swimming pool, or preparing to walk on stage before a thousand people.*
>
> David Jeremiah,
> *Escape the Coming Night*

to be made. A half-hour seems like a short time unless you're waiting for a life-or-death announcement to be made. Then it seems like time has come to a stop.

THE SILENT PREPARATION

Seven angels were given seven trumpets to announce the coming judgments upon the earth (verse 2). Trumpets were used in various ways in Scripture such as calling people to worship (Numbers 10; 1 Chronicles 16). The trumpet was also sounded to prepare people for war (Numbers 10; Judges 3; Nehemiah 4). Those to whom the trumpet blasts were directed needed to know the different sounds of the trumpet and what each meant in order to know how to respond.

THE SAINTS' PRAYERS

A single angel, in a priestly mode, steps forward with a golden censer in his hand (verse 3). Some have suggested this might be the Lord Jesus Christ Himself since He comes forward to offer the prayers of the saints, along with the incense, upon the altar before the throne. I believe these are the prayers offered by the saints in Revelation 6:9-10, those imprecatory prayers offered by the saints who were anxious for God to take vengeance upon the earth. They are prayers for God to take action upon the unrighteous ones upon the earth. The ones offering them are martyrs who were killed for their allegiance to Jesus.

It would appear that the offering of these prayers at the very time the trumpet judgments begin would make those judgments an answer to the martyrs' prayers. The angel filled the censer with fire from the altar and threw it upon the earth, from which "noises, thunderings, lightnings, and an earthquake" came (8:5). The fire represented the judgment of God upon sin on the earth. The prayers of the saints are about to become the punishment of the sinners in verses 7-13.

THE SINNERS' PUNISHMENT

In the final verses of this chapter we have the sounding of the first four trumpets with the last three trumpets coming in chapter 9.

The trumpet judgments sound just before the Second Coming of Christ. Revelation 11:15 indicates that with the sounding of the seventh trumpet comes the announcement that "the kingdoms of this world have become the kingdoms of our Lord and of His Christ." So the seven trumpet judgments introduce us to the section of Revelation which occurs just before Christ returns to earth at His Second Coming to establish His kingdom.

The First Trumpet: a Third of the Trees and All the Grass

Many commentators vacillate back and forth between literal and symbolic interpretations of Revelation. The material in this first trumpet judgment is a good place to note this tendency since it involves dramatic images.

For instance, Walter Scott, one of the great commentators on Revelation with whom I agree most of the time, sees the content of the first trumpet symbolically. He takes the "trees" and "grass" as symbols. He views the "third of the trees" as the leaders of a confederation of nations, and the "grass" as representing people in general. While his conclusions may not be wrong, I cannot be sure how he arrives at them on the basis of "trees" and "grass." That is, when we approach concrete terms in the book of Revelation, how do we know to interpret them symbolically instead of literally—especially since they are no more farfetched than the plagues upon Egypt described in Exodus which we interpret literally?

My conclusion is that we must interpret the effects of these judgments literally unless there is a compelling reason to do otherwise—and the sheer awfulness or unusual nature of the judgments is not such a reason. While hail and fire mingled with blood is a terrifying-sounding reality to consider coming upon the earth, we have already learned that the Great Tribulation is going to be exactly that: a terrifying reality! Ecological devastation upon the earth, and the resulting calamitous impact upon the residents of the earth, will be all too real during this period. It is, after all, a period of judgment.

The Second Trumpet: a Third of the Sea Creatures and a Third of the Ships

While we have no record of "something like a great mountain burning with fire" (verse 8) being thrown into the sea in history, that doesn't mean it won't or can't happen in the future. Indeed, John here uses figurative language when he says "something like." Perhaps he couldn't tell exactly what it was that fell into the sea, but it was "something like" a burning mountain. Many things will happen during the Great Tribulation which have never happened before in the history of the world. Therefore, we should not be surprised at our own shock at some of the things we are reading about. The human tendency is to say, "If it hasn't happened in 5,000-plus years of recorded human history, it can't ever happen."

That is not true; many surprises are in store for any who think that way. Three-fourths of the earth's surface is comprised of oceans, so if a third of that area is turned to blood (.75 x .33 = 25% of the world's oceans), this second trumpet represents extensive judgment upon the earth. Think of the pollution and the death of fish and sea creatures and the resulting loss of food for the human race. The health of the oceans has a dramatic trickle-down effect on the health of our whole planet.

As of January 2016, there were 51,400 oceangoing merchant ships registered. Imagine the shock waves that will hit the shipping industry when 12,850 of these valuable ships are suddenly destroyed with all of their cargo. The loss of life and the economic impact, in addition to further pollution, since many of those ships will be transporting oil and other chemicals. That's what is going to happen when the second trumpet is blown.

The Third Trumpet: a Third of the Fresh Water Supply Poisoned

The judgment of the third trumpet affects fresh water supplies (verses 10-11). The net effect of this judgment is that fresh water is made bitter and undrinkable. Many will die from a lack of fresh water. It has been said human beings can go without food for 21 days, but only 3 days without water. Therefore, many will die as a result of their water supply becoming poisoned. Wormwood grew in Bible lands and had an extremely strong and bitter taste. The book of Jeremiah is filled with references to wormwood to illustrate the bitter time of suffering the residents of Jerusalem experienced in the Babylonian siege of the city.

John clearly says in this case that the cause is a star, or meteor, falling from heaven. In some way it impacts a third of the fresh water rivers and springs of earth, turning their waters bitter and unfit for drinking. History records a great volcano eruption on March 21, 1823, on the Aleutian Islands, which caused all the water in that area to become bitter and unfit for use. Something similar is going to happen again. Whatever the chemical nature of the contamination, it will be sufficient to cause "many men [to die] from the water" (8:11).

The National Geographic Society lists about 100 principle rivers in the world ranging in length from the Amazon River, which is 4,000 miles long, to the Rio de la Plata, which is 150 miles long. The U.S. Geological Survey reports 30 large rivers in the United States, beginning with the mighty Mississippi, which is 3,710 miles long.

One third of these primary rivers and their sources (as well as one-third of all other rivers and springs) will become so bitterly polluted that drinking their water will result in death. It is hard to imagine the resulting chaos on this earth when one-third of the world population has no water to drink-or to use in all the other ways in which fresh water is required.

The Fourth Trumpet: a Third of the Sun, Moon, and Stars Darkened

The fourth judgment is going to affect the sun, the moon, the stars, and the uniformity of day and night (verse 12). These heavenly bodies will be affected in such a way that a third of them will have their normal functions, and apparently even their orbits, changed. It appears that we will have only 16 hours of day and night instead of 24. Jesus Himself predicted there would be signs in the sun, moon, and stars (Luke 21:25).

John saw an eagle ("angel" in verse 13 of the NKJV should read "eagle") flying through the heavens warning the inhabitants of earth about the remaining three trumpets yet to sound. Trumpets five, six, and seven will bring a whole new level of divine displeasure and resulting disaster to the earth. We will see in ensuing lessons a "woe" of locusts and the Euphrates horsemen in chapter 9, the plagues released by God's two witnesses in chapter 11, and the handing over of the earth to the worship of the Beast in chapter 13. Gradually, the earth is being handed over to Satan for the destruction which he will wreak through his agent, the Beast.

> Man has progressed scientifically, medically, and technologically, but he is destroying God's earth in the process. Our grandparents and great-grandparents would have laughed at the thought of purchasing water-treatment systems for their homes, or air-treatment systems for their offices and bedrooms. Even without God's intervention, the earth is being handed over to the greatest polluter of all time, Satan himself.
>
> David Jeremiah,
> Escape the Coming Night

As a conclusion to this lesson, it is worth taking a moment to consider just what it will be like to be on earth when the events we've just read about take place. You lose friends and loved ones in large numbers. You try to contact other loved ones but all the communication systems have been damaged. The news media, what you are able to gain access to, is filled with reports of calamity and destruction and death. And then you begin to hear of a leader who is rising and who claims to be able to marshal the world's resources to restore order and health and resources for living. Every person in the world, except those with spiritual discernment, will be willing to follow his leadership. But his goal will be world domination and worship of himself, not what is best for the world.

The seal judgments see the world ruined by man, the trumpet judgments see the world ruled by Satan, and at the end of the bowl judgments we will see the world reclaimed by the Lord. If you want to see the Tribulation unfold, I highly recommend you do so from the perspective of heaven, not earth.

PERSONAL QUESTIONS

1. How were trumpets used in the context of 1 Chronicles 16? (verse 42)

   a. How will the trumpet be used during the Millennium? (Isaiah 27:13)

   b. Explain the role of the trumpet in the life of the watchman in Ezekiel 33:3-6.

   c. What could serve as a parallel to the trumpet in our day? Who is to play the role of the watchman on the wall?

   d. What serious responsibility does the watchman have? For what will he be held accountable before God? (verse 6)

   e. How will the trumpet be used by an angel in the End Times? (Matthew 24:31)

   f. Knowing a bit about the use of trumpets in the Old Testament, why do you think a trumpet was used to represent the voice of Christ? (Revelation 1:10)

GROUP QUESTIONS

1. What will happen when the seventh seal is opened?

   a. List the first four of the seven trumpet judgments in Revelation 8. Describe what happens after each, and what will be the effects of each.

      1. The First Trumpet:

      2. The Second Trumpet:

      3. The Third Trumpet:

      4. The Fourth Trumpet:

2. Read Numbers 10:1-10 and discuss the following questions:

   a. For what two purposes was Moses directed by God to make two trumpets? (verse 2)

   b. What was to happen when both trumpets were sounded? (verse 3)

   c. And when only one trumpet was blown? (verse 4)

   d. What was the other major use of the trumpets? (verses 5-7)

e. Who was put in charge of using the trumpets in the life of Israel? (verse 8)

f. What was the use of the trumpets as an alarm? (verse 9)

g. What was the use of the trumpets as a memorial? (verse 10)

h. How does the use of the trumpets in Revelation 8:1-13 parallel their use as an alarm in Numbers 10:9?

i. How is the use of the trumpet in 1 Thessalonians 4:16-17 similar to its use in Numbers 10:3?

DID YOU KNOW?

Many of the effects of the four trumpets are ecological in nature. We are already seeing signs and symptoms of ecological pressure that are a harbinger of the disasters to be realized during the Tribulation. Water clean enough for consumption, for instance, is rapidly becoming a scarce resource. Seeking to make a profit from scarcity, international investors are pouring large sums of money into water purification and infrastructure companies. Other investors are quietly buying up water rights throughout the Southwest in anticipation of the coming shortage. These signs serve as a warning about the future to those with eyes to see and ears to hear.

HELL ON EARTH, PART 1

Revelation 9:1-12

In this lesson we are introduced to the current residents of hell.

OUTLINE

Do you believe that hell is a literal place of painful and permanent suffering? If so, you are one of a small percentage of people who do. Even many Christians are not convinced of the reality of hell. John's description of those who live there now just might convince the doubters.

I. **The Unnamed Personality**

II. **The Unlocked Pit**
   A. The Place Dreaded by the Demons
   B. The Place Where Angels Are Retained
   C. The Place Where Jesus Christ Preached
   D. The Place Ultimately Controlled by Jesus Christ

III. **The Unleashed Power of the Pit**
   A. The Description of the Demons From the Pit
   B. The Damage of the Demons From the Pit

IV. **The Unscrupulous Prince**

It's understandable, but to our detriment, that no one likes to talk about hell today in biblical terms. That's understandable for the world—but not for the Church. Unfortunately, many pastors and teachers today skip over references to hell in the Bible and move on to something that will tickle the ears of their listeners.

Most modern religious groups have redefined hell to be a state of mind, or even the life we create for ourselves while on this earth. Is that surprising? Because the Bible presents hell as a literal place that is very unpleasant—a place designed to punish those who lived in rebellion against God while on earth—people avoid it. They even write it out of their theology. Why run the risk of offending people when there are so many other topics to choose from for sermons and messages? The reason is that it's in the Bible, it is therefore true, and therefore we are obligated to teach on it. No one can make something not true simply by denying it.

Chapter 9 of Revelation gives us a glimpse into the horrors of hell. This brief encounter ought to be enough to unsettle anyone's conviction that hell is nothing to be concerned about. Hell on earth during the Great Tribulation is bad, but at least it only lasts a few years. Hell itself is worse, not in the least because it never ends.

By way of review, we are at this point working through the last of the seven seals which secured the title deed to planet earth given by God the Father to Jesus Christ. In the seventh seal are incorporated the seven trumpet judgments, in the seventh of which are the seven bowl judgments. So within the seventh seal itself are fourteen more incremental judgments—seven trumpets and seven bowls. In our last lesson we studied the first four trumpet judgments, and in this lesson we study the fifth (Revelation 9:1-12). At the end of Revelation 8, at the conclusion of the fourth trumpet, an eagle announces, "Woe, woe, woe to the inhabitants of the earth . . . ." We would think the inhabitants of earth are suffering woe already based on the previous judgments—but it only gets worse with the fifth trumpet.

Think of the fifth trumpet this way—as if every prison in the world threw open its doors and set free the vilest offenders known to man. That's what the fifth trumpet releases—only the doors are the doors to hell and the offenders are demonic instead of human.

The Unnamed Personality

We have read about stars falling to earth in earlier parts of Revelation, but the one described in 9:1 is different—it has a human personality. The star is referred to as "him" and "he" in verses 1-2. We have seen stars refer to people earlier in Revelation (1:16, 20), so this is not unusual.

> *It is quite difficult to express the effect produced by the sight of the whole atmosphere filled on all sides and to a great height by an innumerable quantity of these insects, whose flight was slow and uniform and whose noise that of rain.*
>
> Harry Ironside

This unnamed personality who falls to earth in the fifth trumpet judgment is undoubtedly Satan himself. He is allowed by God to open the doors to the "bottomless pit" (9:2) so that the demons of hell can go out upon planet earth in force. A more illustrative reading of the perfect tense of the Greek verb in verse one would be, "I saw a star which had already fallen to earth." The star, the angel that has already fallen from heaven to earth, is none other than Lucifer: "How you have fallen from heaven, O Lucifer . . ." (Isaiah 14:12, 15). Another reference to Satan's fall is Jesus' comment that He "saw Satan fall like lightning from heaven" (Luke 10:18). And in Revelation 12:7-9 we have an important passage about the dragon (Satan) being cast out of heaven. It is possible that Revelation 12 is actually an expansion of what is mentioned in 9:1. This would not be unusual in the structure of Revelation at all since we know there are parenthetical chapters spaced throughout the book (specifically, between the sixth and seventh seals, trumpets, and bowls). So it is possible that chapter 12 is a commentary on Satan falling from heaven which is mentioned in its chronological place in 9:1.

THE UNLOCKED PIT

Satan is given permission to open the "bottomless pit" (verse 2). When he does, the sky is darkened by the smoke that pours forth from it—smoke that conceals the reality of what is actually coming forth.

The Place Dreaded by the Demons

If demons don't even want to go into the bottomless pit of hell, how bad must it be? When Jesus encountered demons in the man who lived in the land of the Gadarenes (Luke 8), the demons begged Him not to send them to the pit (Luke 8:31). They wanted to remain free to roam; they didn't want to be sent into the abyss where they would be confined. There are many angels (demons) that are not free, that are confined to the abyss at the present time. So Jesus sent them into a nearby herd of pigs which the demons drove into the sea.

The Place Where Angels Are Retained

In Jude 6 we learn about the angels who are confined in the abyss, the bottomless pit, at the present time: "And the angels who did not keep their proper domain, but left their own abode, He has reserved in everlasting chains under darkness for the judgment of the great day." So angels who rebelled against God (heaven being their "proper domain") have been assigned to the abyss until their judgment and permanent casting into the "everlasting fire prepared for the devil and his angels" (Matthew 25:41).

The Place Where Jesus Christ Preached

The abyss is the place Jesus Christ preached between His death and resurrection. He went there to proclaim victory over death to the fallen angels. First Peter 3:18-19 describes this post-Calvary visit of Christ to the "spirits in prison." He didn't preach the Gospel to them. Rather, He went to announce that He was going to be victorious over death. They had hoped that the cross was the end of Christ, that their leader Satan had succeeded in putting to death the Redeemer of mankind. But His message to them was that He had won and they had lost.

The Place Ultimately Controlled by Jesus Christ

The "key to the bottomless pit" (9:1) was given to Satan. That means he did not have control over or access to the abyss. Because Jesus has the keys of "Hades and of Death" (Revelation 1:18), the keys are His to give as He will. And as part of the judgment God is bringing on the earth, He gives Satan the keys so as to unleash demonic power in the last part of the Great Tribulation.

It is extremely important to remember in all of our understanding about the world as we know it that God is in control. Satan, demons, and evil are on a leash which ultimately is held by the hand of God. If He did not restrain the powers of evil in our world, the human race would have self-destructed millennia ago. Because the last years of the Great Tribulation is a period of intense judgment on the human race, these evil forces are let loose—God extends the leash further than it has ever been extended before.

THE UNLEASHED POWER OF THE PIT

The smoke arising from the pit has two-fold importance. First, Jesus speaks of hell as a place where the fires never go out (Mark 9:48; Luke 3:17). Second, the demons are pictured as locusts coming up out of the pit, which I understand can appear as a huge cloud of smoke when they swarm by the millions. So there is literal as well as figurative meaning. We know these aren't real locusts because they do not harm the vegetation (9:4), they have a king (9:11; real locusts have no king; Proverbs 30:27), and God promised never to release swarms of locusts in judgment again after the locust swarms in Egypt (Exodus 10:14). The use of locusts, as an image of demons swarming over the earth is an effort to paint a picture of something with which we are very unfamiliar.

The Description of the Demons From the Pit

The locusts John saw had a number of very unusual characteristics representing the lion, the horse, the scorpion, the man, and the locust.

1. They Are Imperial Creatures

    Their shape was like "horses prepared for battle" (9:7). While some cultures use the word for *horse* to describe the appearance of the locust, John is not focusing on how they look. He is talking about the strength and imperial nature of the locusts. We have already discussed the role of strength and courage of the horse in ancient culture as a creature charging fearlessly into battle. The demons are coming out prepared for battle.

2. They Are Invulnerable Creatures

    They had golden-like crowns on their heads (9:7), the *stephanos* of the victor. They are pictured as going forth with the intent to win in battle.

3. They Are Intelligent Creatures

    Their faces, "like the faces of men," speak of their intelligence. They are not dumb insects going out for battle; they are highly organized and intelligent forces of evil.

4. They Are Intriguing Creatures

    The locusts' hair is said to be like women's hair, which speaks of their seductiveness. Women's hair in the ancient world was a tool of seduction, and just as some women employed their beauty to get what they wanted, so the locusts will have seductive skills in accomplishing their goals.

5. They Are Inhuman Creatures

    Their lion-like teeth (9:8) speak of their power, their ability to rip and destroy their prey.

6. They Are Indestructible Creatures

Their armor was like iron (9:9) meaning they were indestructible. Demons are only vulnerable to the Name and power of Christ.

7. They Are Impressive Creatures

This is a powerful, final description John gives. Cooped up for thousands and thousands of years, when the demons burst forth from the pit their wings sound like horses and chariots running into battle (9:9). One description I read compared the sound of a swarm of locusts to that of pouring rain.

The Damage of the Demons From the Pit

What are the characteristics of the attack of these demons on the population of planet earth near the end of the Great Tribulation?

1. Painful

The damage inflicted by the demons over the earth is like the sting of a scorpion, among the most painful experiences known to man (9:10). The pain inflicted on mankind by the demons will be excruciating.

2. Protracted

Their power to inflict painful suffering on mankind will last five months (9:5, 10). Imagine an extended scorpion sting, the pain of which persisted and persisted. The agony of living in a world overrun by demons will seem unending—though its duration is five months. Their power was not to kill but to torment. Many who have experienced excruciating pain have said that, in the midst of it, they would rather have died. This pain will be that bad.

3. Personal

Their attack is upon those who are not the elect of God (9:4). The 144,000 Jewish evangelists are excluded, as are those Jews and Gentiles they have won to Christ. Revelation 22:4 indicates

> *Hitler was demon-possessed: He changed a generation and temporarily altered the course of history. What will be the result of countless thousands of demons running unchecked throughout the earth during this time of the Tribulation? It will be a Dachau/Buchenwald type of experience for those who are left to endure it.*
>
> David Jeremiah,
> *Escape the Coming Night*

that in the heavenly city those who are the Lord's will have His Name on their foreheads. These are the ones who are exempt from the attack of the demons.

4. Perpetual

Revelation 9:6 says men will "seek death and will not find it . . . desire to die, and death will flee from them." Many will desire in that day to use death as an escape from the torment of the demons, but will be unable to succeed. While the demons themselves are limited to five months of torment, the pain will go on beyond that.

THE UNSCRUPULOUS PRINCE

The ruler of the demons is *Abaddon* (Hebrew), or *Apollyon* (Greek). This is the devil, the ruler of all fallen angels.

Everything we have studied in these lessons are warnings to those who read them. The images of hell are supposed to warn us about a real place called hell—and alert us to take steps not to find ourselves there. Hell is a place of fire and smoke populated by creatures whose only purpose is the infliction of pain and suffering.

There is only one way to avoid the pain of hell. Embrace the One who announced to hell that He had defeated death so you might live forever with Him.

PERSONAL QUESTIONS

1. Read Revelation 9:1-12.

   a. How does John describe the demons from the pit?

   b. Break down their seven characteristics and what each represent.

   •

   •

   •

   •

   •

   •

   •

   c. What are four characteristics of the damage they will cause?

   •

   •

   •

   •

d. Who will be protected from this? (Revelation 22:4)

2. Read Isaiah 14:12-15. The passage describes the king of Babylon but serves as typology of Satan who empowers both ancient, and future (Revelation 14:8; 16:19; 17:5; 18:2, 10, 21), Babylon.

   a. What happened to "Lucifer, son of the morning"? (verse 12)

   b. Identify Lucifer's five acts of rebellion in verses 13-14:

      1. I will

      2. I will

      3. I will

      4. I will

      5. I will

   c. When Satan was cast out of heaven, where was he sent? (verse 15)

   d. How does this provide background for what we've learned in this lesson?

GROUP QUESTIONS

1. In your experiences, do people mostly want to talk about hell, in biblical terms, or not? Why or why not?

   a. Why is it important to talk about hell, and the reality of it, even though it might be an uncomfortable subject?

2. What does an eagle announce at the end of Revelation 8? What does it mean?

   a. Describe in detail what will happen after the fifth trumpet.

   b. What is the "bottomless pit" that is referred to in Revelation 9:2?

   c. Talk about the four depictions of the pit listed in the lesson.

      •

      •

      •

      •

3. Read Luke 8:26-38 and talk about the following questions:

a. What was the spiritual condition of the man Jesus encountered? What was his appearance? (verse 27)

b. What evidence was there of supernatural influence in the man's life? (verse 29)

c. How many demons inhabited the man? (verse 30)

d. Who is doing the speaking in a demon-possessed person? (verses 28, 30-31)

e. Where did the demons not want to be sent? (verse 31)

f. How is the "abyss" parallel to the "bottomless pit" of Revelation 9:2?

g. Where did Jesus allow the demons to go rather than going to the abyss? (verse 32)

h. What was the immediate impact of the presence of evil on the pigs? (verse 33)

i. How was the behavior of the man and the pigs similar? How did they both give evidence of supernatural influence?

j. What was the immediate impact of the absence of demonic possession on the man? (verse 35)

k. The community had lived in fear of the man. Why were they also in fear of Jesus? (verse 37) (Which is to be feared more: evil, or One who is stronger than evil?)

l. Why is this significant?

DID YOU KNOW?

The Greek word behind the English "demon possessed" is *daimonizomai*—to be under the power or influence of a demon. The Greek word is used to describe some who were severely influenced and whom Jesus delivered (Matthew 4:24; 8:16, 28, 33; 9:32; 12:22; 15:22; Mark 1:32; 5:15; John 10:21). In some cases the demons had taken over the person's rational sensibilities (Luke 26-38), but in other cases the demon(s) was responsible for lesser afflictions (Matthew 12:22). That is, being influenced by a demon is not the same as being totally possessed by a demon. Demons can gain a foothold (opportunity to influence) wherever sin is tolerated and they are not resisted (Ephesians 4:26-27; James 4:7).

HELL ON EARTH, PART 2

Revelation 9:13-21

In this lesson we see the effects of the largest army in history.

OUTLINE

Modern warfare has changed dramatically in recent years. There is more emphasis on technology and less emphasis on the foot-soldier. But an army will arise in the future that defies the imagination and will overwhelm the world based on its sheer size alone.

I. **The Demand**
   A. The Tools of God's Judgment Are Prescribed by the Demand
   B. The Time of God's Judgment Is Prescribed by the Demand
   C. The Targets of God's Judgment Are Prescribed by the Demand

II. **The Details**

III. **The Description**
   A. The Worship of Those Who Are to Be Judged
   B. The Works of Those Who Are to Be Judged

W e are in the process of unfolding the judgments of the seventh seal of the title deed to planet earth given to Jesus Christ by Him who sits on the throne of heaven. That seventh seal, as we have seen, contained seven trumpets of judgment which fall upon planet earth during the Great Tribulation, the last half of the seven year period of judgment on earth. The first four of the trumpet judgments are found in Revelation 8, and numbers five and six are set forth in Revelation 9. In our last lesson we studied the fifth trumpet, the releasing from hell of a cloud of demons which afflict the world with indescribable pain.

In this lesson we will examine the sixth trumpet judgment, a command from God to release judgments which will take the lives of a third of the earth's population (Revelation 9:13-21).

THE DEMAND

It is important to notice in verse 13 that the command to judge comes from the horns of the golden altar which is before the throne of God. This fact takes us back to Revelation 6:9-11 where we saw the souls of Tribulation martyrs crying out to God for vengeance upon those who took their lives on earth. They were told to "rest a little while longer" until the number of martyrs was completed. We saw the prayers of those martyred saints ascending to the Lord in 8:3, and now in the sixth trumpet judgment we see their prayers answered as God releases an army of judgment to march across the earth.

The Tools of God's Judgment Are Prescribed by the Demand

The four angels about to be released upon the earth are not to be confused with the four good angels of Revelation 7:1. There are good angels and bad angels in the Bible, and the four we encounter in 9:14 are of the bad sort. Good angels (7:1) restrain evil, but bad angels (9:14) release evil. These angels have been "bound at the great river Euphrates," chained up and prevented from acting—until now. The release of these angels can be compared with the release of the locusts in 9:3.

The River Euphrates is the most frequently mentioned river in the Bible. It originated in the Garden of Eden (Genesis 2:14) and flowed south for 1,780 miles through Mesopotamia (Babylon and later Persia). The first sin, the first murder, the tower of Babel, Babylon itself—all happened at or near the River Euphrates. God's judgment has always been associated with this river.

The Time of God's Judgment Is Prescribed by the Demand

The four evil angels have been kept in waiting for "the hour and day and month and year" of their release (9:15). Their place in the plan of God is precise. The only thing missing is the date which is known only to God. No dates concerning End Time events have been given to the angels or to mankind, not even to Jesus Christ Himself (Matthew 24:36). But the fact that the hour of the angels release is set means that God has a date. If we knew the date we would orient our lives around that date rather than around Him, so He has not revealed it.

The Targets of God's Judgment Are Prescribed by the Demand

The targets of the four angels' terrors are one-third of the remaining inhabitants of the earth. Revelation 6:8 began with 25 percent of the world's population being killed. Now a third of the remaining 75 percent (or another 25 percent) is going to be killed. So with the completion of this judgment nearly half the world's population has perished. Not since the flood in Noah's day has such a huge portion of the human race perished in such a brief interval of time.

THE DETAILS

Verse 16 says that this decimation will be accomplished primarily by an army of "two hundred million" persons. Some people cite Revelation 5:11 to show that John often uses huge numbers to indicate an innumerable amount—that we aren't to read "two hundred million" as a literal number. But I believe it is a number to be taken literally—an army of 200 million soldiers.

Revelation 16:12 describes the judgment associated with the sixth bowl which is to be poured out, which involves the drying up of the River Euphrates. So we have the sixth trumpet and the

When John wrote this prophecy there were not even two hundred million people on earth. It is estimated that by the year 2025 the population of China will be at least 1.4 billion. It is not difficult to imagine that there could be a soldier for every seven thousand civilians, producing an army of 200 million. This number is almost twice as many troops as the Allied and Axis powers combined, when they were at peak strengths in World War II.

David Jeremiah,
Escape the Coming Night

sixth bowl each having to do with the Euphrates. Many expositors of Revelation believe that, because the seven trumpet judgments are contained in the seventh seal, and the seven bowl judgments are contained in the seventh trumpet, that many of the trumpet and bowl judgments are occurring not consecutively but contemporaneously. That is, the sixth trumpet and the sixth bowl, both focusing on the River Euphrates, would be separated by very little actual time in terms of the three-and-a-half years of the Great Tribulation.

The reason this is important is because the drying up of the River Euphrates would make it possible for "kings from the east" (16:12) to make their way westward, toward Israel. And there is a country to the east of the Euphrates that could field an army of 200 million persons: China. Obviously, the transporting of that many soldiers from China to the Middle East would be impossible by airplane or ship. Interestingly, a great deal of road-building activity has been underway for years by China along the borders with her southern and western neighbors which will make it possible someday to move millions of people quickly into the Middle East. Regardless of how "peaceful" the world scene might appear at the moment, the stage is being set for another world-level conflagration in the future.

The descriptions of the soldiers and even their horses speak volumes about the kind of destruction they will bring with them—fiery breastplates, horses' heads like lions, and fire, smoke and brimstone coming from the horses' mouths. We have to wonder if, from John's perspective 2,000 years ago, some of the imagery he applied to describing what he saw was a foretelling of modern effects of nuclear warfare. Some students of prophecy think John is describing, in an elementary fashion, implements of modern warfare which would be used in a worldwide war in the future.

Whatever the exact manifestation of war that occurs, we do know this: The largest army in the history of the world is going to cross a dried-up Euphrates and bring destruction to the world.

THE DESCRIPTION

We now turn to identifying those who will be the recipients of the judgments brought by this massive army upon mankind. Remember —when this happens, the Church will have already been raptured. There are believers on earth however—the 144,000 Jewish evangelists and those who have believed through their witness. However, many of them will have already been martyred by this time. Some have gone underground; others have fled for their lives. But most of them, if they remain faithful to the Lord and refuse to take the mark of the Beast, will be persecuted and martyred. However, just because there are few genuine Christians to be found doesn't mean worship isn't still going on.

The Worship of Those Who Are to Be Judged

The worship of demons (idolatry) will be in full force during this period (verse 20). Satan will have energized millions of people to worship him through worship of the Antichrist. Just as we see in our own day millions of people involved in religious worship toward false religions, the same false religions will be active during the Tribulation. But anything that is not the worship of the true and living God is idolatry, the worship of Satan.

Notice the downward progression, the deterioration, of worship during the Tribulation. They start out worshiping idols of gold, and then digress to silver, to brass, to stone, and to wood. There is only a downward spiral in idolatry. As I look around the Christian world today, I see supposed believers who look like they are worshipers of the Tribulation age. People today who worship money and material things, or who worship their edifices of stone and wood, are no less guilty of idolatry than those who will worship these inanimate things in the Tribulation.

The Works of Those Who Are to Be Judged

Worship always dictates works. Worship God and you'll do good works. Worship gold, silver, brass, stone, or wood and you'll eventually do the works of the flesh. John describes four kinds of works of those worshiping idols in the Tribulation (verse 21).

1. Murders

We can see the devaluing of human life in some cultures where the true God is not worshiped. And, unfortunately, we can see it in our own. More attention seems to be paid today to the rights of the murderer than to the victim and his family. People are taking others' lives today over trivial matters— randomly and arbitrarily. The number of murders portrayed on television and

> *Stupefying and hallucinatory drugs have been associated with sorcery and witchcraft for ages, yielding to their users strange visions and hallucinations, which they could interpret as oracles for the guidance of their clients. Also, they divested their users of the control of their own minds, making them easily available for possession and control by evil spirits.*
>
> Henry Morris

in movies has dulled our consciences to the horrible act of taking a human life. If it is this way today, think what it will be like in the spiritually dark days of the Great Tribulation.

2. Drugs

The word *sorceries* in 9:21 is a translation of the Greek word *pharmakon* from which we get our word *pharmacy*. Its original meaning was related to the combination of drug-based occult practices. Astrology, witchcraft, and divination were a gateway to demon possession. In the Tribulation there will be rampant use of drugs and widespread occult practice. Can you see the Tribulation being an outgrowth of modern culture today where these two works are everywhere present? Losing control of one's mind through the use of mind-altering drugs becomes a natural spiritual way for the devil to come in and take control.

3. Fornication

The third prominent sin of the Tribulation will be rampant immorality. The word *porneia* refers to all types of sexual activity outside the bonds of marriage. Every institution today except the Church—and in some cases even the Church—is promoting in one way or another the breakdown of God's standards of sexual purity. Children are being taught and equipped in public schools to engage in "safe" sex. Colleges and universities have men and women sharing bathrooms in dormitories. Psychologists and psychiatrists focus more on personal fulfillment than on purity and loyalty. And that's not even considering the media—sex is everywhere you look. Just as sex dominated the cultures of ancient Greece and Rome before their demise, so it will come to characterize the culture of the world before its demise.

4. Dishonesty

Thefts will be characteristic of the Tribulation culture, not only in terms of the scarcity of the necessities of life and people stealing food and other goods from one another, but also in the breakdown of honesty across the board. Man's conscience, without the sanctifying presence and restraining influence of the Holy Spirit, will become dead. Truth will become a thing of the past. There will be no standard for what is honest and what is dishonest; the lines will have disappeared. People will do whatever is right in their own eyes (Judges 17:6). From the point of view of honesty, anarchy will reign—the absence of any moral order to guide men's behavior.

I hope you never have to find out, but what would you do if you found yourself living in a situation like that? War going on around you, moral anarchy ruling your land, drug use, sexual perversion, and the occult taking place on every street corner. What would you do? We would think that anyone finding themselves in such a world gone awry would fall to his or her knees and cry out for the grace and mercy of God, cry out to be saved. But such is not the case. Twice John tells us that the people he saw in his vision "did not repent" (9:20, 21).

The heart of man is not changed by punishment. His behavior may be temporarily altered because of the fear of pain, but only the Gospel can lead a person to true repentance. It's possible that very few people will turn to God in those final days and be saved. That is why today is the day of salvation. Make sure you have responded to the Gospel today before a day comes when it may be impossible.

PERSONAL QUESTIONS

1. To what would you attribute mankind's willingness to worship inanimate objects created by their own hands—idols? (Revelation 9:20)

2. Describe the difference between the four angels in Revelation 7:1 and the four angels in Revelation 9:14. What did each group do in John's vision?

   a. What is the purpose of the angels in Revelation 7:1?

   b. Who is the target of the angels in Revelation 9:14?

3. What are the four kinds of works of those worshiping idols in the Tribulation that John describes? Expand on each.

   •

   •

   •

   •

4. How does God feel about the death of the wicked? (Ezekiel 33:11)

    a. For what reason did God withdraw His favor from Israel? (Ezekiel 5:11)

    b. What would God rather the wicked do? (Ezekiel 18:23, 32)

    c. What does God want for all humanity? (1 Timothy 2:4; 2 Peter 3:9)

    d. How can this encourage us to spread the Gospel before the anguish of the Great Tribulation?

    e. Rather than waiting until calamity strikes, what are Christians called to do? (Isaiah 55:6-7)

GROUP QUESTIONS

1. Read Isaiah 44:12-20 and answer the following questions:

   a. What kind of care and energy did ancient idol-makers invest in their craft? (verses 12-13)

   b. The same wood used to create a "god" is used for what else? (verses 14-16)

   c. What irony do you find in verses 16-17 regarding the dual uses of the same piece of wood?

   d. What is the source of the blindness that prevents the idol-maker from seeing his folly? (verse 18)

   e. Who was given the commission by God to declare this spiritual blindness and deafness in Israel? (Isaiah 6:1-8)

   f. Describe the condition Israel would experience. (Isaiah 6:9-10)

   g. And for how long? (Isaiah 6:11-13)

h. What evidence of this blindness and deafness do you find in Matthew 13:13-15?

i. Jesus spoke in _____ in concert with God's decree of blindness on Israel. (Matthew 13:13a)

j. The idol-maker threw half his wood in the _____ (verse 16) and _____ the other half. (verse 17)

k. If a person held an idol in his hand, what is actually in his hand? (verse 20)

l. How does this section from Isaiah illuminate Revelation 9:20?

2. If you feel comfortable doing so, share your notes from the personal questions on God's will for the wicked:

a. How does God feel about the death of the wicked? (Ezekiel 33:11)

b. For what reason did God withdraw His favor from Israel? (Ezekiel 5:11)

c. What would God rather the wicked do? (Ezekiel 18:23, 32)

d. What does God want for all humanity? (1 Timothy 2:4; 2 Peter 3:9)

e. How can this encourage us to spread the Gospel before the anguish of the Great Tribulation?

f. Rather than waiting until calamity strikes, what are we called to do? (Isaiah 55:6-7)

DID YOU KNOW?

The Euphrates River is one of the oldest rivers in recorded history, being one of the four rivers emanating from the river flowing out of Eden (Genesis 2:10-14). Because it is the longest and most important river in western Asia, in Scripture it is referred to as "the great river" (Genesis 15:18; Deuteronomy 1:7). Originally, the Euphrates was the eastern boundary of the land promised by God to Abraham (Genesis 15:18; Deuteronomy 1:7; Joshua 1:4). Under kings David and Solomon, partial and temporary success was gained in incorporating that region under their rule. The Euphrates originates in Turkey and flows through Syria into Iraq where it joins its sister river, the Tigris, before emptying into the Persian Gulf.

THE DIVINE INTERLUDE

Revelation 10:1-11

*In this lesson a message of encouragement and hope
appears in the midst of judgment.*

OUTLINE

It would take a less-than-honest person to look around our world
and not secretly wonder if evil has gotten the upper hand. If that
is true now, how much more true might it be during the Great
Tribulation? A message of reassurance comes when it is most needed
in a dark world.

I. **The Messenger From Heaven**
   A. The Descent of This Messenger From Heaven
   B. The Description of This Messenger From Heaven
   C. The Deeds of This Messenger From Heaven

II. **The Message From Heaven**
   A. A Seven-Fold Message
   B. A Sealed-Up Message
   C. A Sworn Message

III. **The Mandate From Heaven**

A s we begin chapter 10 of the book of Revelation, we find ourselves in a parenthesis between the sixth and seventh trumpet judgments. The sixth trumpet sounded and resulted in a mighty army, 200 million strong, being released to continue the worldwide destruction which constitutes God's judgment on humanity. As we pause following the sixth trumpet, we realize there is but one trumpet left to blow, and the time of Jacob's trouble will be over. That seventh trumpet contains the seven bowl judgments which bring to a close the most devastating time of trial ever known to the human race.

With all the darkness Satan is unleashing on the earth we might wonder if God has lost control, whether Satan has gotten the upper hand. Chapter 10, the focus of this lesson, reassures us that God is very definitely in control of the final days of the Great Tribulation. The parenthesis between the sixth and seventh trumpets does the same thing as when we use a parenthesis in writing—it conveys necessary information that is not part of the flow of the immediate narrative. Revelation 10:1-11:14 is an interlude. It tells us something in between the sixth and seventh trumpets which we need to know about grace and mercy and love. There are interludes between the sixth and seventh seals, trumpets, and bowls. In each case God, breaks in to give us needed insights on the story line.

> *Where were you, God, when the baby died? Where were you when the missionaries were massacred? Why do bad guys seem to win and good guys lose? The time is coming when God is going to deal with those questions once and for all. Revelation 10:7 says, "...the mystery of God will be accomplished, just as he announced to his servants the prophets." We will see the puzzle of the ages solved.*
>
> David Jeremiah,
> *Escape the Coming Night*

The parenthesis of chapter 10 is a message from heaven that reveals grace in the midst of judgment on earth.

THE MESSENGER FROM HEAVEN

In his vision, John sees a messenger descending from heaven who brings a message of hope to the earth, a beam of light that pierces the dark days of judgment (verses 1-3a).

The Descent of This Messenger From Heaven

Note first that this is a good angel sent from heaven, not a fallen angel like the four who were stationed at the River Euphrates (9:14). This is the third time we have met this angel (7:2; 8:5). While there is no small measure of debate over his identity, my own conviction is that it is none other than the Angel of Jehovah, the Lord Himself.

God often visited Israel in the person of the Angel of Jehovah (Genesis 18:1; Exodus 3:2; Judges 2:4; 6:11-12, 21-22; 2 Samuel 24:16). The Angel of Jehovah is a theophany, or the preincarnate Christ. Because the Angel of Jehovah often appeared to Israel, I believe it is not unusual that we would find Him appearing in the "time of Jacob's trouble" (Jeremiah 30:7), the Great Tribulation. When we read John's description of the Angel, I believe it confirms His identity as the Angel of Jehovah.

The Description of This Messenger From Heaven

1. Clothed With a Cloud

   This Angel is robed in that which is always associated with deity—a cloud. On Mount Sinai, God came down in a thick cloud (Exodus 19:9). He led the Israelites through the desert in a cloud (Exodus 16:10). When He spoke with Moses it was in a cloud (Exodus 24:15; 34:5). When Christ ascended to heaven it was in a cloud (Acts 1:9). And when He returns it will be in a cloud (Revelation 1:7). The clouds are the chariots of God (Psalm 104:3).

2. Crowned With a Rainbow

   The rainbow on the Angel's head reminds us of the rainbow associated with the throne of God (Revelation 4:3), as well as the rainbow which was God's promise never to destroy the world again through a flood (Genesis 9:13). This Angel's rainbow suggests that He has come from the presence of God.

3. Covered With Glory

   The Angel's shining face fits the face of Jesus Christ (Matthew 17:2; Revelation 1:16). And Malachi 4:2 even refers to the Lord as the "Sun of Righteousness."

4. Carried on Feet Like Pillars of Fire

   His feet "like pillars of fire" are similar to the feet of Christ in Revelation 1:15, "like fine brass, as if refined in a furnace."

The Deeds of This Messenger From Heaven

This Angel comes to deliver a message, holding a little book (scroll) in His hand (verses 2-3a).

1. Holding the Opened Book

   In the Greek language of verse 2, the word *opened* is in the emphatic position—like when we write something in all caps for emphasis. The last time we saw a book in Revelation it was the seven-sealed book in the hand of God, the title deed to planet earth. And Christ took off the seals and opened the book. And now He holds a book again, and one that is opened. I believe it is the same book, now lying open in His hand, since the seven seals have been removed.

2. Standing Upon the Sea and the Earth

   With one foot on the sea and the other foot on the land, Christ speaks "with a loud voice, as when a lion roars." His stance is a picture of His sovereignty over all the earth, and the book a sign of His right to possess the earth as ruler over it. His message is one of reassurance and comfort: "Do not fear. I am in control."

3. Crying With a Loud Voice as a Lion

   His voice matches His appearance: clothed with a cloud, a rainbow on His head, face shining like the sun, feet as burnished brass—and a voice like the roaring of a lion. Often in Scripture the voice of a lion is associated with the voice of a ruler (Proverbs 19:12; Joel 3:16). Even Satan, in his counterfeit role of ruler, goes about like a roaring lion (1 Peter 5:8). This Angel is the same as the Lion of the tribe of Judah whom we met in Revelation 5:5.

THE MESSAGE FROM HEAVEN

This mighty, divine Angel from heaven takes a posture of authority and roars like a lion—and is immediately answered by seven thunders reverberating across the earth (verses 3b-4).

A Seven-Fold Message

I have to wonder if the seven thunders of the voice of the Lord in Psalm 29 are the backdrop for the seven thunders in (verse 3b): powerful, full of majesty, breaking the cedars, dividing the flames of fire, shaking the wilderness, making deer give birth, and stripping the forests bare (Psalm 29:4-9; see also Job 37:5). The powerful sound of this seven-fold message going forth reaffirms the majesty and authority of the speaker.

A Sealed-Up Message

A strange thing happens to John when he hears the message. He is about to write it down but is suddenly told to "seal up the things which the seven thunders uttered, and do not write them" (10:4). Some things are secret and known only to God (Deuteronomy 29:29). I am not ashamed to say that I have no idea what the seven-fold message was contained in the seven thunders—and neither does anyone else. The only thing I can conclude is that it is something too awful for us to hear.

A Sworn Message

The Angel of Jehovah now does what some have considered to be an unusual thing: He swears an oath "by Him who lives forever and ever . . ." (verse 6). Many have pondered this, wondering why God would need to swear by anyone since there is no one greater than God. Hebrews 6 offers a parallel situation which sheds light on this passage: "For when God made a promise to Abraham, because He could swear by no one greater, He swore by Himself" (Hebrews 6:13). Since there is no one greater than God, God swears by Himself.

What Jehovah swears is "that there should be delay no longer" (10:6). Remember the cries of the souls under the altar who asked, "How long, O Lord . . . until You judge and avenge our blood . . .?" (Revelation 6:10) At that time, the Lord's answer was that they should wait "a little while longer." But now He is saying that the wait is over. Judgment is about to be completed; there will be no more delay in the fulfillment of the seventh trumpet God is often accused of delay, but His plan is always on time (2 Peter 3:3-4).

The mystery of God is the focus of the oath that the Angel of Jehovah swears (10:7). But what is the mystery? What mystery will be finished when the judgments are complete? While there are many opinions among Bible students as to what the mystery refers to, I believe it is simply the plans God had revealed to His servants the prophets to conquer evil and establish righteousness on the earth. An honest person would have to admit that it is a bit of a mystery as to why Satan has been allowed to work evil in the affairs of men for thousands of years. For the longest time, the evidence would seem to suggest that Satan, not God, was in control. This is the mystery of God referred to here. But it is not a mystery to God, only a mystery to us. God has had a timetable and a purpose for all of time which He is bringing about. The end of the mystery will be when He takes control once again, banishes Satan and evil, and completes His plan of the ages.

> *Does it not seem strange that Satan has been allowed for six thousand years to wrap and twist his coils around the world, to work evil and spoil and mar the work of God?...Is it not a mystery why God, the God of righteousness and holiness, allows evil to go unpunished and His own people to be crushed and broken on every hand? Truly this is the mystery of God. ... God bears with evil till the hour of judgment arrives, when He will avenge the cry of His elect, and come out of His place to punish the wicked... evil, now tolerated and allowed, will be openly punished. The mystery is at an end. Christ is about to reign.*
>
> Walter Scott

There is hope in that message, hope that every person needs. When we look around our world and wonder whether evil has not gotten the upper hand, all we have to do is remember that God always has the upper hand. For those who are battling for their lives in the middle of the Great Tribulation, they need to know that God is about to bring the greatest mystery of the age to a conclusion and prove it was never a mystery to Him. He and His righteousness will reign forever and ever.

THE MANDATE FROM HEAVEN

John is, for the first time, asked to play a part in one of the visions that are unfolding before him (verses 8-11). And a strange part it is! He is told to approach the Angel of Jehovah and take the small book from Him. When he asks for it, he is told to eat it (10:9). Almost the exact same thing happened to Ezekiel. He was told to consume the message God was giving him, which he did. And he had the same digestive problems John was about to have (Ezekiel 2:8-3:3). The message tasted sweet, but didn't sit too well in his stomach.

Remember, the book is the book of the seven seals of judgment. John is told not so much to eat it physically as to assimilate it into himself, to absorb its message—to learn and understand it. As he does so, its message will become bitter to him. That very thing happened to me as I studied the book of Revelation in preparation to preach the messages on which this study guide is based. Just as I would find the study of God's plan sweet to my taste, the reality of judgment to come upon this world would turn it to bitterness in my inner man. Prophecy is sweet to the taste but bitter in the application.

John is told that he must yet preach "about many peoples, nations, tongues, and kings" (10:11). John is warned not to preach this message of judgment unless he has assimilated it into his own life. Too often we traffic in undigested truth. Passively we preach about judgment when it ought to bring tears to our eyes. Only when we have internalized the message will our preaching have power and authority. Anyone who preaches only that which is sweet like honey is missing the rest of the counsel of God. The same Gospel that sends me to heaven will send another to hell. The preacher who does not preach all the message of God does a disservice to those who listen.

You may not be a preacher, or even a teacher. But if you're a mom or dad or employer or associate or friend, then the word that came to John is for you. When you share the Gospel with others, make sure you share the whole Gospel. And the only way to make sure you'll speak it all is to digest it all first. When the judgment of God begins to fall on this earth, make sure that no one to whom you have spoken is unaware of the dire consequences of rejecting the Gospel.

PERSONAL QUESTIONS

1. What use did God make of a cloud in the exodus of the Hebrew slaves from Egypt? (Exodus 13:21; 14:19)

   a. Why did God appear to Moses enveloped in a thick cloud at Mt. Sinai? (Exodus 19:9, 16)

   b. When Moses disappeared into the cloud for forty days, what was the cloud a symbol of? What was Moses "going into"? (Exodus 24:18)

   c. Even when the tabernacle was built in the wilderness, how did God manifest Himself to Israel? (Exodus 33:9-10)

   d. How did the cloud govern the movement of the people in the wilderness? (Exodus 40:34-38)

   e. What did the cloud become a symbol of for the people?

f. Why are symbols important in the spiritual life? Why do we need "things" on which to fix our attention and our understanding?

g. What symbols did Jesus use as a recorder in Luke 22:17-22? What did the symbols stand for?

h. Why are clouds a symbol of God's strength? (Psalm 68:34; see Psalm 19:1)

i. For what purpose did a cloud appear at the top of the Mount of Transfiguration? (Matthew 17:5)

j. Why do you think Jesus said (twice) that the Son of Man would come "on the clouds of heaven"? (Matthew 24:30; 26:64; see Luke 21:27) Could He not come as easily on a cloudless day?

k. How do these images provide some background for what we learned about the Angel of Jehovah in this lesson?

GROUP QUESTIONS

1. What reassurance do we have that God has not lost control of the world to Satan?

2. Read Revelation 10:1-11:4 and talk about the following questions:

   a. What would be a good description of these verses? Why could this be considered an interlude?

   b. What does John see in Revelation 10:1-3a?

   c. What is the description of the messenger from heaven?

   •

   •

   •

   •

d. What reasons have we to believe that this angel is the Angel of Jehovah?

e. What are three of the deeds of the messenger from heaven? (Revelation 10:2-3a)

*

*

*

f. What is the significance of each deed?

g. What was the message from heaven? (Revelation 10:3b-4)

*

*

*

DID YOU KNOW?

The Angel John saw coming down from heaven had a "rainbow on his head" (Revelation 10:1). The rainbow has great theological significance as a covenant sign from God to man through Noah—the sign of God's promise never again to destroy the world by a flood (Genesis 9:8-17). The two times a rainbow appears in Revelation it is as a circle: around the throne of God (4:3) and around the head of an angel (10:1). On earth, when we see the arc of a rainbow that disappears below the horizon, we are seeing only a portion of a rainbow. From the right vantage point in the atmosphere, rainbows are a complete circle—exactly like the ones seen by John in heaven.

THE TWO WITNESSES

Revelation 11:1-14

*In this lesson the Law and the Prophets
return to judge Jerusalem.*

OUTLINE

The city of Jerusalem is the most embattled city in history—but her most dramatic days are yet to come. The eyes of the world will be focused on the words and works of two men who will call Jerusalem to account for her sinful ways. And the entire world will see what happens when they do.

I.   **Measure the Temple**

II. **The Two Witnesses**
  A. Their Personalities
  B. Their Prophecies
  C. Their Power
  D. Their Persecution
  E. Their Preservation

In this lesson, we approach what many scholars believe is one of the most difficult chapters to interpret in all the New Testament. But I believe it is possible to read Revelation 11 with understanding if we keep three presuppositions in mind. First, this chapter is essentially a "Jewish" chapter of Scripture. It focuses on Jerusalem, the temple, and the Jews' place in End-Time activity. Second, this is a prophetic chapter, not a historical chapter. The temple had been destroyed in A.D. 70, before John wrote Revelation. Finally, this chapter is to be interpreted literally—people, numbers, places, and events.

Having established those preliminary foundations, we shouldn't have any problems gleaning the riches contained in Revelation 11.

MEASURE THE TEMPLE

We are still in the interlude, or parenthesis, between the sixth and seventh trumpet judgments (Revelation 11 is a continuation of Revelation 10). The first two verses set the stage for what is about to take place: the temple in the holy city of Jerusalem. There were five temples in Jewish history. The first was Solomon's temple, destroyed by Nebuchadnezzar in 587 B.C. Next was Zerubbabel's temple, built when the Jews returned from captivity in Babylon. It was desecrated and destroyed in the second century before Christ. The third temple was built for the Jews by Herod the Great, the temple in existence during Jesus' ministry and the apostles' ministry as described in Acts. This was the temple destroyed by the Romans in A.D. 70. These are the three temples of history. Yet to be built are the Tribulation temple described in Revelation 11 and the Millennial temple described in Ezekiel 40-43.

The temple in existence during the Tribulation period will be rebuilt by the Jews sometime during the Tribulation days—but not as an act of faith. It will be part of the Zionist political movement which has dominated Israel since her reorganization as a nation in 1948. In fact, we are told in 2 Thessalonians 2:3-4 that the Antichrist will set himself up in the temple of God in Jerusalem in order to take the place of God in Jewish worship. The Antichrist who makes a covenant with Israel in order to curry favor with her will ultimately break that covenant and defame the temple just as Antiochus Epiphanes defamed the temple of Zerubbabel in the second century B.C.

When John is told by the Angel to measure the dimensions of the temple, it is a precursor to judgment. A *rod* in Scripture is always an indication of coming judgment. Measuring the temple had nothing to do with determining its size; it is a matter of circumscribing the realm of judgment which God is going to exercise against the idolatrous worship taking place in the temple under the leadership of the Antichrist. God is saying through John that the Jewish temple court is going to be judged.

John's experience at the beginning of the chapter sets the stage for what is going to follow in the next verses.

> *The two witnesses are a great illustration of a divine truth: The man of God in the will of God is immortal until he has finished the work God has given him to do.*
>
> David Jeremiah,
> *Escape the Coming Night*

THE TWO WITNESSES

Verse 3 introduces us to two witnesses who, I believe, will come on the scene as soon as the Antichrist makes a covenant with Israel at the midpoint of the seven year Tribulation. They will preach the Gospel throughout the Jewish world. There are five key points to note concerning the two witnesses:

Their Personalities

The two prophets are real human beings, not symbols of something else. Wearing sackcloth, they minister as prophets in mourning over the spiritual condition of Israel. Drawing from an Old Testament prophecy in the book of Zechariah, the two witnesses are called olive trees and lampstands, signifying their ministry of light in the power of the Holy Spirit.

Their Prophecies

In verses 3, 6, 10, and 18 *prophecy* and *prophets* are mentioned. Prophecy doesn't always mean telling the future (foretelling). Prophets also speak forth the Word and will of God (forthtelling). The fact that there are two of them raises the question of their identity since God often dispatched people in teams of two.

Most commentators, and I agree, believe that one of the prophets is Elijah sent back to earth, for the following reasons:

1. Malachi the prophet predicted that Elijah the prophet would come before the Second Coming to prepare the way of the Lord (Malachi 3:1-3; 4:5-6). The Passover service held by Orthodox Jews today has a cup which is called Elijah's cup. They know that Elijah must come before the Messiah comes. John the Baptist came in a manner prefiguring Elijah before Jesus' first coming, but he himself said he was not Elijah (John 1:21). Therefore, Elijah is still to come.

2. Elijah did not experience death; he went to heaven in a whirlwind of fire (2 Kings 2:9-11). Therefore he could come back to earth and die since he never died physically.

3. One of the two witnesses' signs during the Tribulation is they make it stop raining—the same thing Elijah did during the reign of King Ahab (1 Kings 17:1; Revelation 11:6).

4. The period of drought in Elijah's day was the same duration as the time of the ministry of the witnesses here in Revelation 11 (1 Kings 17:1; Revelation 11:3; Luke 4:25; James 5:17-18)—three-and-a-half years (42 months, 1,260 days; Revelation 11:2-3).

5. This would not be the only time Elijah has appeared after he left earth. He appeared with Jesus on the Mount of Transfiguration (Matthew 17:3). And I believe the other person who appeared with him at that time is the second witness of Revelation 11—Moses. (Some believe it will be Enoch, since he, like Elijah, was translated to heaven without dying; Genesis 5:24.)

There are five reasons I believe the second witness is Moses.

1. As noted above, Moses and Elijah have already appeared together in ministry (Matthew 17:3).

2. While withholding rain is consistent with Elijah's former ministry, turning "waters to . . . blood" is consistent with Moses' former ministry in Egypt (Revelation 11:6; Exodus 7:14-24).

3. Moses was buried but no one knew where, possibly so that someday he could be restored to life and ministry in the Tribulation (Deuteronomy 34:5-6).

4. Satan contended with Michael for the body of Moses (Jude 1:9). It's possible that Satan knew of God's future plan for Moses in the Tribulation, and he and the angel Michael got in a dispute over the disposition of Moses' body.

5. Moses and Elijah represent the Law and the Prophets. And for a period of time that is distinctly Jewish as the Great Tribulation is ("the time of Jacob's trouble"), it makes sense for representatives of the Law and Prophets to appear to the Jews.

Their Power

For them to survive the antagonism of the Jewish nation, the two witnesses will have to be imbued with power from God.

1. The Power of Their Preaching

There will be five realms in which their power is manifested:

a. They will declare that Jesus Christ is Lord of all the earth by virtue of His ability to withhold rain.

b. Like prophets of old, they will not shrink from declaring that sin is sin among the Jewish leaders.

c. They will testify concerning the character of the judgments being experienced.

d. They will preach against the Beast who blasphemes God (Revelation 13).

e. They will preach against the spiritual hypocrisy of the Jewish leadership.

2. The Power of Their Plagues

Verse 5 indicates they will have the power of immediate judgment, the power of life and death over those who try to harm them. The power of their plagues is seen three ways.

a. Death

They will be able to protect themselves from any sort of physical harm. Fire proceeding from their mouths seems unusual to us, but that's what the Bible says will happen (11:5). The reason I think this may happen just like Scripture portrays it is that the story of Elijah and the servants of the wicked King Ahaziah in the Old Testament (2 Kings 1) reveal how Elijah called down fire from heaven on 100 of the king's servants.

b. Drought

We have already mentioned their power to withhold rain during the Tribulation.

c. Disease

They have the power "to strike the earth with all plagues, as often as they desire."

Their Persecution

Verses 7-10 reveal the persecution which will be directed toward the two witnesses—persecution which leads to their (temporary) death.

1. The Death of the Witnesses

In verse 7 we have the first of 36 references in Revelation to "the beast that ascends out of the bottomless pit." The Beast and his False Prophet are paired against the two witnesses. The witnesses were untouchable until they had finished their assignment from God—"When they finish their testimony...." God gave them 42 months to preach and, when their ministry was complete, the Beast was able to gain access to them—but not before.

2. The Display of Their Bodies

When they were killed by the Beast, the witnesses' bodies were allowed to lie in the street for three-and-a-half days. Such hatred has been generated toward these men that they are not even accorded a burial, something the Jewish Law required immediately after death—even for a criminal (Deuteronomy 21:22-23). It was a great offense in Judaism to allow a dead body to lie unburied. But they lay in the street for the entire world to see.

> *The exposure of their dead bodies tells of a most extraordinary malignity and spite...It shows at once a devilishness of unwanted intensity in the people, and a terribleness of efficiency in the Witnesses in provoking a fiendishness and resentment so monstrous and unrelenting that it could not be placated by their death, but continued to reek and vent itself upon their lifeless remains after they were dead.*
>
> Joseph Seiss

Remember—this is in the future when television cameras will record the scene for the whole world.

3. The Delight of Their Enemies

Residents of earth, and especially Jerusalem, will turn their death into an occasion for a holiday. The "torment" of the two prophets has ended which is cause for a celebration. It is hard to believe how deeply the depravity of man runs, but here we see it in full force. Servants of God are killed and the deaths celebrated like a holiday.

Their Preservation

They are allowed to lie in the street for three-and-a-half days in order to establish the certainty of their death. And while they were genuinely dead for that time, they are not dead for all time, for God restores them to life.

1. Their Resurrection

Courtesy of satellite broadcasts, all over the world people will see the two witnesses resurrected from death to life. The Beast will not be able to kill them again. Indeed, their first death was probably just to demonstrate their power over death through their resurrection, as in the case of Christ.

2. Their Rapture

   Not only are they resurrected, they are raptured as well. God calls them to heaven after their ministry is concluded on earth (11:12). Interestingly, the Greek text doesn't say "a" cloud took them to heaven, but "the" cloud—which I believe to be the cloud of the Shekinah glory of God. God sends His glory down to usher His two faithful witnesses to heaven (for Elijah, the second time).

3. Their Revenge

   Immediately after their departure "there was a great earthquake." A tenth of the city was destroyed and 7,000 people died (11:13). These who died, the Greek text says, are "men of renown." There may be a clue to their identity in Jude 1:15-16 where we are told that, when the Lord returns, He executes judgment on those who have used their great words to gain advantage over others. Perhaps the 7,000 who die are leaders in Jerusalem who have led others astray by their positions of prominence.

Verse 13 says "the rest . . . gave glory to the God of heaven." But I don't think they were saved. I think they repented out of fear, not faith. The difficulties of the moment caused them to call out to God, but it wasn't genuine. They were like those atheists in foxholes who call out to God when the bullets are flying, then forget Him once peace is restored.

My prayer is that you will be like the two witnesses—men and women of great faith—not like the rest who call on God out of a fearful and insincere heart. God's grace will come to an end one day, and the Law and Prophets will return. Now is the time for all people everywhere to place their faith in Him.

PERSONAL QUESTIONS

1. What preliminary foundations must we establish to fully understand Revelation 11?

2. Why is John told to measure the temple?

3. Two periods of time are mentioned in Revelation 11:2—42 months and 1,260 days. Since a biblical year was counted as 360 days, how many years do each of the two time periods refer to?

   a. What is the similarity between this number of years and "the middle of the week" (a week of years) in Daniel 9:27?

b. What similarity do you find between Revelation 11:7—the appearance of the beast at the end of the three-and-a-half years—and the appearance of the "prince who is to come" in "the middle of the week"? (Daniel 9:26-27)

c. What does the "prince who is to come" (Daniel 9:26) do to establish peace with Israel? (Daniel 9:27a)

d. And what does the prince do "in the middle of the week"? (Daniel 9:27)

e. Having broken his covenant with the Jews, what is likely to happen to them in the second half of the seven-year Tribulation? (compare Jeremiah 30:7, Daniel 12:1, and Matthew 24:21)

GROUP QUESTIONS

1. Read Revelation 11:1-14 and discuss the following questions:

   a. Based on your own opinions, share who you think the two witnesses might be. Why do you think so?

   b. What reasons does the lesson give for who they might be?

   c. When do the two witnesses likely come to earth?

   d. What is their purpose?

   e. What are the five key points to note concerning the two witnesses? Why are each of these points important?

      •

      •

      •

      •

      •

   f. What two types of power will the witnesses possess and how will they demonstrate each?

g. What does the persecution of the witnesses include?

-

-

-

h. What are the three steps of the preservation of the witnesses?

-

-

-

2. Summarize and talk about some of the highlights you have learned in this study, and how each piece of information has changed your perception of End Times.

DID YOU KNOW?

The Dome of the Rock in Jerusalem is an Islamic shrine that was completed in A.D. 691 on the Temple Mount, the site of the third temple (Herod's Temple, destroyed in A.D. 70) in Israel's history. (The first temple was built by Solomon, the second by Zerubbabel following the restoration from Babylon.) During the Crusades the Dome was used as a church but reverted to Muslim hands when Jerusalem was recaptured by Saladin in 1187. Jewish tradition holds that the rock outcropping in the floor of the Dome is the top of Mount Moriah where Abraham went to sacrifice Isaac (Genesis 22) and is the foundation stone—the site of the Holy of Holies in Herod's Temple.

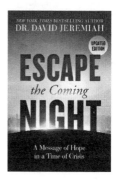

Escape the Coming Night

Tragedy and violence surround us ... political debates divide our society ... our world seems to be coming apart at the seams. So is there any hope for peace in our time? In *Escape the Coming Night*, Dr. David Jeremiah narrates the book of Revelation, answering this question and more, for those who are willing to listen to what God declares about the final days and His coming reign.

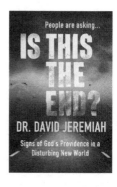

People Are Asking ... Is This the End?

Never has there been so much moral decay in our world. With each new occurrence, people are asking ... *Is This the End?* In this book, Dr. Jeremiah answers two questions: "Is this the end for America?" and "Is this the end for the world?" He covers events happening today—terrorism and the "anything goes" society—and prepares readers for what is to come—the Rapture of the Church.

Agents of the Apocalypse

What if the players of the End Times were out in force today? In *Agents of the Apocalypse*, Dr. Jeremiah explores Revelation through the lens of its major players—the martyrs, the dragon, the Victor, and more. He opens each chapter with a dramatization and ends each with "The Scripture Behind the Story," explaining how we should interpret and apply Revelation to our lives today.

Agents of Babylon

Babylon has been a symbol of evil since the beginning of time. And nowhere in the Bible can we see this exemplified more than in the book of Daniel. In *Agents of Babylon*, Dr. Jeremiah brings the characters and prophecies of Daniel to life, projecting them into the future to show us how to live in the present and have hope as these End-Time events unfold.

For pricing information and ordering, contact us at

P.O. Box 3838
San Diego, CA 92163
(800) 947-1993
www.DavidJeremiah.org